• PRAISE FOR •

THE LEADER HABIT

"In *The Leader Habit*, Martin Lanik distills the last twenty years of psychological research into an engaging read and a fabulous leadership 'how to' that's peppered with practical tips. Any aspiring leader or coach would benefit from making this book their new *reading* habit."

—KATE BRAVERY,
Global Practices Leader, Talent at Mercer

"*The Leader Habit* provides a clear and engaging set of principles anyone can use to increase their success at work and in life. It shows how to change simple habits in a way that creates significant and lasting improvements. Employees will appreciate how the book demystifies what it takes to go from being an individual contributor to a leader. Managers will value the simple, focused tips for improving leadership effectiveness in their current roles. And human resource experts will appreciate the book's foundation on sound, evidence-based practices. In my book *Commonsense Talent Management,* I discussed how the most powerful achievements are often the result of consistently applying basic and easy-to-understand concepts. *The Leader Habit* exemplifies this principle–simple is powerful."

—STEVEN T. HUNT, Ph.D.
Senior Vice President of Human Capital
Management Research for SAP SuccessFactors

THE
LEADER
HABIT

THE LEADER HABIT

MASTER THE SKILLS YOU NEED TO LEAD IN JUST MINUTES A DAY

MARTIN LANIK

AMACOM

AMERICAN MANAGEMENT ASSOCIATION

New York • Atlanta • Brussels • Chicago • Mexico City • San Francisco
Shanghai • Tokyo • Toronto • Washington, D.C.

Bulk discounts available. For details visit:
www.amacombooks.org/go/specialsales
Or contact special sales:
Phone: 800-250-5308
E-mail: specialsls@amanet.org
View all the AMACOM titles at: www.amacombooks.org

American Management Association: www.amanet.org

Some names, identifying details, and events have been changed to protect the privacy of individuals.

Library of Congress Cataloging-in-Publication Data

Names: Lanik, Martin, author.
Title: The leader habit : master the skills you need to lead--in just minutes a day / by Martin Lanik.
Description: New York : American Management Association, [2018] | Includes bibliographical references and index.
Identifiers: LCCN 2017051455 (print) | LCCN 2017054819 (ebook) | ISBN 9780814439357 (ebook) | ISBN 9780814439340 (hardcover)
Subjects: LCSH: Leadership.
Classification: LCC HD57.7 (ebook) | LCC HD57.7 .L365 2018 (print) | DDC 658.4/092—dc23
LC record available at https://lccn.loc.gov/2017051455

About AMA
American Management Association (www.amanet.org) is a world leader in talent development, advancing the skills of individuals to drive business success. Our mission is to support the goals of individuals and organizations through a complete range of products and services, including classroom and virtual seminars, webcasts, webinars, podcasts, conferences, corporate and government solutions, business books, and research. AMA's approach to improving performance combines experiential learning—learning through doing—with opportunities for ongoing professional growth at every step of one's career journey.

10 9 8 7 6 5 4 3 2

To everyone who thinks reading this book will improve your leadership skills.

It will . . . if you put it into practice.

CONTENTS

Prologue: Laura's Story xi

Part I: How It Works

CHAPTER 1: Leadership Is a Series of Habits 3

CHAPTER 2: The Leader Habit Formula 21

Part II: Build Your Leadership Skills

CHAPTER 3: How to Sustain Practice 45

CHAPTER 4: From 5-Minute Exercise to Full-Blown Skill 65

CHAPTER 5: Starting Your Leader Habit Workout 83

Part III: Exercises That Develop Your Skills

CHAPTER 6: Getting Things Done 101

Planning & Execution 101

Skill: Manage Priorities 102

Skill: Plan and Organize Work 105

Skill: Delegate Well 108

Skill: Create Urgency 111

Solving Problems & Making Decisions 113

Skill: Analyze Information 114

Skill: Think Through Solutions 116

Skill: Make Good Decisions 119

Skill: Focus on Customers 123

Leading Change 126

Skill: Sell the Vision 127
Skill: Innovate 129
Skill: Manage Risk 132
CHAPTER 7: Focusing on People 137
Persuasion & Influence 137
Skill: Influence Others 138
Skill: Overcome Individual Resistance 141
Skill: Negotiate Well 144
Growing People & Teams 148
Skill: Empower Others 148
Skill: Mentor and Coach 151
Skill: Build Team Spirit 154
Interpersonal Skills 157
Skill: Build Strategic Relationships 158
Skill: Show Caring 161
Skill: Listen Actively 164
Skill: Communicate Clearly 166
Skill: Speak with Charisma 169

Part IV: Encourage New Skills in Others

CHAPTER 8: Motivating Change 175
CHAPTER 9: Coaching Leader Habits 197

Acknowledgements 221
Notes 223
Index 233

Prologue: Laura's Story

Laura, an emergency room nurse at a hospital that hired me to provide leadership training for its employees, had always considered herself to be a good leader. As the best nurse in the ER, she prided herself on leading her patients to better health outcomes, and she frequently acted in an informal leadership capacity for her peers. She believed she would make a great nurse manager, certainly better than most of the military-style dictators she had reported to so far in her career. But Laura kept getting passed over for management positions, and she was frustrated that no one seemed to regard her as a leader. Attending a leadership development program seemed like a good way to prove that she was ready to become a manager, so she signed up for my session. She wasn't sure how much she would actually learn—it was corporate training, after all—but she thought the credentials would help her finally get promoted. If not, she planned to quit nursing and become a real estate agent.

What Laura didn't realize was that she had come to resemble the military-style dictators she loathed. Her colleagues saw her as argumentative, sarcastic, always pushing her own agenda, dismissive of others' opinions, a poor listener, emotionally volatile, and difficult to manage—not the qualities of an effective leader, to say the least.

Laura wasn't consciously choosing to be negative or difficult to work with. She didn't show up for her shifts intending to make sarcastic remarks, fight with coworkers, or get upset and aggressive when people disagreed with her—she was just acting that way without thinking. She had fallen into a pattern of negative behaviors that she repeated automatically. These behaviors had become so ingrained that she wasn't even aware of how she was perceived by her peers and the hospital's leaders. Six years of long hours, high stress, and a combative culture at work had turned Laura into a burned-out, negative person—and she didn't even realize it.

Laura arrived for my leadership development program with the same negative attitude. Years of experience with corporate training had taught her to keep her expectations low. She was skeptical that she would learn anything new or become better prepared for a management position, but she was willing to sit through a few days of "soft-skills" lectures so that she could put "Leadership Development Training" on her résumé.

When Laura walked into the first session, she was surprised to find that the program wasn't set up like other training programs she had attended. Instead of presenting a series of lectures and workshops, with textbook-style reading materials thrown in for good measure, the program focused on building positive leadership habits through simple, 5-minute daily exercises. Still, Laura's automatic response was sarcasm: "So I'll become a better manager by practicing these trivial exercises for five minutes a day? Sure. Whatever you say." It seemed too simplistic and too good to be true, but she decided to go along with it. "Okay," Laura thought, "let's jump through these hoops and get this over with." Little did she know that she was about to change her life.

The Change Came in Two Months

Laura began her leadership development with a single exercise designed to help her learn to ask open-ended questions: *After realizing that you want to ask a question, start it with the words "what" or "how."* All she had to do was practice this behavior once per day. Being a competitive, driven individual, she took on the challenge, but she quickly discovered that she didn't have time to stop and consciously think about asking open-ended questions during her hectic workdays in the emergency room. To make sure she didn't forget to practice her exercise, Laura wrote a reminder on her hand each day before starting her shift: "Ask what/how questions."

The exercise felt awkward in the beginning, but every day, as Laura practiced asking open-ended questions, she learned something new. She noticed for the first time how diverse the opinions of her colleagues were, and she realized that she enjoyed hearing them. She also realized that her colleagues were much more receptive to what she had to say if she first asked about their perspective before giving her own opinion. She began developing better relationships with everyone in the ER, even colleagues she had struggled to get along with before. With every repetition of the exercise she felt more confident, and she found that her skill at asking open-ended questions was rapidly improving.

After about two months, Laura realized that she didn't need to write the reminder on her hand anymore. She was asking good, open-ended questions in every conversation. In fact, she often caught herself doing it without having to think about what questions to ask. The skill that had once felt awkward and difficult had become so natural and easy that it was now an automatic behavior. It had become a habit.

The Usual Holiday Argument

Laura's new habit didn't just change the way she behaved at the hospital; it carried over into every part of her life.

Each year, December brought more than snowstorms and Christmas spirit to Laura and her two sisters. This was the time of year that the three sisters got in heated, bitter arguments about Christmas gifts.

Their annual discussion about how much to spend on each other and their nieces and nephews had become an unpleasant holiday tradition that always ended in yelling, name-calling, hurt feelings, crying, and regrets. Every year, Laura, who didn't have children of her own and was fortunate to have a higher income, insisted on buying presents for everyone, while her sisters wanted to draw one name for a gift exchange.

This year, however, the sisters' conversation about gift-giving took an unexpected turn. As soon as the topic of the gift exchange came up, Laura's new habit took over. She still preferred to buy gifts for everyone, but instead of immediately shooting down her sisters' idea, as she had done every time in the past, she asked, "How come you want to draw names?" This simple question completely changed the course of the discussion. For the first time in years, Laura and her sisters had a deep, honest conversation about what each of them wanted, and why. Instead of shouting over each other, they were listening to each other. Because of Laura's question, she and her sisters were able to reach a gift-giving agreement that suited each of their needs. Afterward, one of Laura's sisters hugged her tight and said, "That was different!"

Better Habits, More Success

Over time, Laura's new habit led to many new personal and professional successes. She got the promotion she wanted. She overcame her burnout and began to love her profession again. She became the leader she had always believed herself to be. She improved her relationships with her colleagues, friends, and family members. As a result, she is happier and more confident today than ever before. All because of a 5-minute exercise.

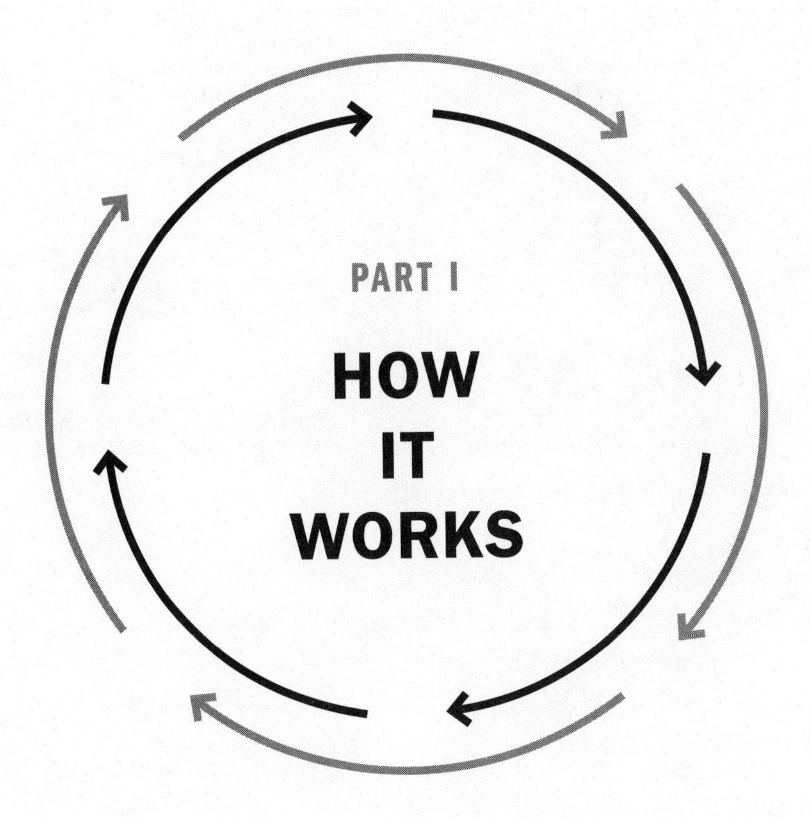

PART I

HOW IT WORKS

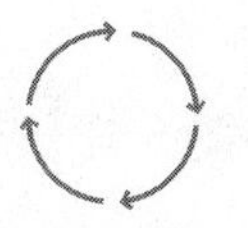

CHAPTER 1

Leadership Is a Series of Habits

People with strong leadership skills succeed in business and life. Whether you are coaching a junior baseball league, leading a church group, raising a family, building a start-up, managing a team in an established business, or running a multibillion-dollar global company, being an effective leader makes it easier to achieve your goals.

This book is about becoming a better leader by forming better habits, as Laura did. The method is simple: you identify a leadership skill you want to master, such as active listening, then you practice that skill through a short, focused exercise every day until it becomes a habit. I call this the Leader Habit Formula.

The Formula is different from other leadership development programs. Instead of relying on theoretical knowledge and classroom-based learning, which are the standard methods for most leadership training, and for educational and self-improvement programs in general, the Formula is a continuous process that helps you develop leadership skills through deliberate practice. This approach is based on scientific observations about how people most effectively learn new skills and how powerfully habits affect our behavior. The better your leadership habits, the better you will perform as a leader—and the more successful you will be.

But before we can talk about the Formula in detail, we first have to understand what habits really are.

What Is a Habit?

Psychologists define a habit as an *automatic behavior.* That means that we don't think about our habits—they seamlessly happen in response to a given cue with little or no conscious effort, and often without us being aware of them.[1] Habits make us more efficient, save us precious mental energy, and allow us to focus on other things—like pondering the meaning of life or fantasizing about our next beach vacation.

People often think of habits as bad behaviors they must struggle to eliminate. For instance, you may wish to quit smoking, drink less, or take the stairs instead of the elevator. But not all habits are bad. In fact, you already hold many positive habits that enhance the quality of your life—you can walk, read this book, drive a car, count money, read a balance sheet, book a flight on the Internet, swim, ski, play a musical instrument; you understand language and can have a conversation with your colleagues and friends, to name just a few common habits.

Some habits you acquired through deliberate practice. You went to school to learn how to read and count, how to understand financial statements, how to manage projects. Through practice, these skills became automatic, and now they are processed in your unconscious mind. Other habits you picked up unintentionally—perhaps your parents insisted on certain daily behaviors, like eating breakfast before leaving the house in the morning. You internalized these behaviors as habits, too. No matter how you acquired your habits, they literally changed your brain.

Your brain consists of billions of cells called neurons. With every new experience, these neurons create new connections with other neurons.[2] It is through these connections that neurons communicate as they share information in the form of an electric impulse. Two neurons that are connected fire together—the electric impulse that started in one neuron gets carried to its neighbor. Your brain records the new experience as a circuit of particular neurons that fire together in the same pattern.

With every repetition of the same experience, that particular neural circuit fires again and again, making it stronger and more easily accessible among all other competing memories and thoughts your brain is storing and processing. The stronger the neural circuit becomes, the more automatically it is retrieved and processed.

It is this *automaticity* that turns behaviors into habits. Automaticity is the ability to perform a task without having to focus on its every detail, and it develops with practice. You know you have reached automaticity when you can do two tasks in parallel at the same time. Perhaps the best example of automaticity is driving a car. When you first started learning how to drive, you had to focus on every detail of the task—the gas pedal, clutch, brake, steering wheel, rearview mirror, lights, turning signals, and so on. But now that driving has reached automaticity, you don't consciously think about these details; you just drive effortlessly and you can listen to the radio or carry on a conversation at the same time.

No One Consciously Chooses to Be a Bad Leader

If you paid close attention to Laura's story, you noticed that, before she changed, Laura wasn't consciously choosing to be a negative, rude person. She didn't wake up each morning thinking whom she could pick a fight with, whose idea she could denigrate, or which sarcastic remark she could make. Laura got in the habit of acting this way without any conscious awareness that she was doing it. Once the bad habits set in, she was just reacting to everyday events with her repertoire of negative behaviors without thinking. Automaticity had taken over her interactions.

Laura's experience is a common one. In fact, I haven't met a single person in my entire career who was consciously choosing to be a bad leader. When leaders act badly, it's usually out of a bad habit—something about the situation makes them unconsciously slip into a bad behavior without realizing it.

For example, imagine that you walk into your employee's office to ask him for something you need. His office door is open but he is in the middle of a conversation with a customer. Your employee is not establishing eye contact, a nonverbal sign letting you know that he wants to finish the conversation before getting to you. Do you rudely interrupt the conversation? Or do you politely wait until your employee and the customer are finished?

Researchers at New York University posed a similar question. More importantly, the researchers wanted to see if they could make people automatically slip into bad habits without being consciously aware they were doing so. Could they get people to act rudely and interrupt the conversation? To test this, the researchers designed a simple experiment. University students came into the laboratory thinking they would complete two short tests of language ability. In the first test, students were given several lists of scrambled words and asked to put each word scramble into a grammatically correct sentence as quickly as they could. An example would be: "pizza—you—like—do," and the grammatically correct sentence would read: "Do you like pizza?" After students completed the first test, they were told to find the researcher, who would give them instructions for the second test. The researcher would be waiting in another room pretending to have a conversation with a colleague. As soon as the student walked into the second room, the researcher, without making eye contact with the student, secretly started a stopwatch to time precisely how long it would take the student to interrupt the pretend conversation.

Unknown to the students, the first language ability test was a setup to see if they would automatically slip into bad habits. Some students completed a sentence scramble test that contained negative words, like *annoying, aggressive, blunt,* and *rude,* which we'll call the *rude group*. Other students completed a similar sentence scramble test, but this time the words in the test were positive, like *respect, polite,* and *courteous*; we'll call this the *polite group*.

Who was more likely to interrupt the researcher—students in the rude group or the polite group?

If you guessed the rude group, you are correct. In fact, 67 percent of students in the rude group interrupted the conversation, as compared to only 16 percent of students in the polite group. Although students in the rude group weren't aware of it, their brains unconsciously processed the meaning of the negative words in the sentence scramble test, which in turn made them automatically slip into the bad habit of interrupting others.[3]

A similar discovery was also made by researchers at the University of Southern California. This time the bad habit of interest was speaking loudly in a quiet setting. What would it take for students to slip into the negative habit of being loud in a quiet research laboratory? It turns out that simply seeing a picture of a sports stadium did the trick. For students who frequented sporting events at a stadium, the picture triggered the habitual response of speaking louder.[4] They didn't need to be in the presence of typical instigators to raise their voice, such as an argument, or to overcome obstructing sound.

"The Unbearable Automaticity of Being"

The two research studies described above demonstrate just how easy it is for us to slip into bad habits without realizing it. Although interrupting another person and speaking loudly in a quiet place are just two common examples, every aspect of your personal and professional life has the potential to be influenced by automatic, habitual patterns of behavior. From the moment you wake up until the moment you fall asleep, you carry out the same, consistent routines. And many of your routines are completely automated—you don't even know you do them, or you might call them something esoteric like intuition or a sixth sense.

Odds are that you follow the same routine every morning in precisely the same order. It probably goes something like this: After the alarm goes off, you start the coffee machine, make your bed, take a shower, brush your teeth, get dressed, eat breakfast, get in your car, and drive to work taking the same route. Once you get to work, you take the elevator to the fourth floor, greet the receptionist, walk straight to your office, open your computer, go through new emails, review your schedule, get another cup of coffee, scroll through your social media feeds, read the news, and answer a few emails before heading to your first meeting. You have probably been repeating this routine five days a week for the past ten to twenty years since joining the workforce—and all of it is habit-driven behavior.

I borrowed "The Unbearable Automaticity of Being" from the title of a 1999 article published in *American Psychologist*. In this eye-opening article, the two psychologists laid out the research evidence that challenged the basic assumption of modern psychology—that people consciously process and analyze information around them and use it to make deliberate decisions and choices about their behavior. The research evidence showed, however, that much of people's everyday behavior is not a result of their conscious decision-making or deliberate choice.[5] Your brain unconsciously processes information around you and, in many cases, automaticity takes over and you respond without conscious awareness. In other words, you are a creature of habit.

In fact, nearly half (43 to 47 percent) of your everyday behavior at work and in life is habitual and processed automatically, without your conscious awareness.[6,7] The reason for this is the limited capacity of the human brain's *conscious processing* power. A person can be aware of (consciously process) only about 110 bits of information per second. Yet even the simplest daily tasks demand a lot of mental power. For example, it takes sixty bits of information per second just to decode speech and understand the meaning of the words on this page.[8]

Even the way you read the words on this page is a result of a well-established habit. You are automatically reading from left to right, top to bottom. You dno't sonud out idinvduial letrets, but rtaehr you amuotatlicaly exractt meniang from wrods. Notice how easily you read the previous sentence, in which most words were misspelled? That's because your brain automatically processes each word as a whole. So long as the first and last letters are in the correct place, your brain fills in the rest.

When you reach the last line of this page, your brain will automatically cue up another habit—to turn the page. Do you know how many pages you already turned since picking up this book? Probably not, because you turned them automatically, without conscious awareness. You most likely didn't think to yourself, "I am on the last line of this page. In about two seconds I will reach with my right hand to the top right corner of the page, place my thumb and index finger in the page, give it a gentle squeeze to lift the page, then quickly move my right hand underneath the page, push the page to the left, catch the page with my left hand, and then return my right hand back to hold the book."

Since you are right now focused on decoding the meaning of words and sentences on this page, most of your conscious processing power is consumed. You are not aware, for instance, that your breathing has slowed, that your hand is getting tired from holding the book, or that the chair you are sitting on is a little too hard to be comfortable. But your brain is taking in all this information and analyzing it without your awareness, and it adjusts your body automatically. Perhaps you lowered your hand to rest it on your leg, or you switched position on the chair to redistribute your weight. Whether you consciously realize it or not, you are constantly responding to cues around you with numerous well-practiced habitual responses.

Automaticity Is Not Only Bearable, It's Beneficial

Not long ago, I met an interesting gentleman at a dinner party in New Orleans; let's call him Scott. Eight years ago, Scott was one of twenty people invited to hear a pitch from an up-and-coming software company. The pitch meeting resembled an episode of *Shark Tank* or *Silicon Valley*—a bunch of young hotshots passionately describing how their disruptive technology was going to change the world, in this case the world of Human Resources (HR). "There was something about these guys," Scott recalled. "Their passion was contagious and spread through the room like wildfire until it hit the back row where I was sitting. All of a sudden, I got this overwhelming feeling in my gut that I had to join them."

At the time, Scott was employed in his father's HR consulting business, which had five full-time employees, a few contractors, and steadily generated about $2 million in annual revenue. The firm offered mainly outsourcing services of the mundane parts of HR, like payroll and benefits, to a small portfolio of midsized companies. Scott's father had built a solid business, and Scott had spent his early adult years preparing to take over when his father eventually retired.

After the pitch meeting, Scott became convinced that the software he had just seen was the future of HR, and he couldn't shake the feeling that he and his father needed to pivot their business to support it. It was a huge risk. Few people had even heard of the new software, and only a handful of companies were using it. Plus the software was competing in a mature market dominated by two behemoth providers, so gaining market share wouldn't be easy. And yet, Scott convinced his father to get on board, and together they pivoted their small consulting business to piggyback onto this new software application. Moving forward, their business would only offer HR outsourcing services that directly plugged into this new software. Despite the risk, Scott was certain the move would pay off.

Scott's intuition was correct. Today, the software Scott first saw eight years ago is a well-known player in the HR market. The once-small start-up is now a fast-growing, $1.5 billion publicly traded company. By joining forces with the company early on, Scott's own business has grown to eight hundred employees and $500 million in annual revenue. Was it the luck of being at the right place at the right time? Or was Scott's intuition the result of habit?

Scientific studies suggest that intuition is, in fact, nothing more than internalized expertise—another form of automaticity and habit. For example, it has been documented that expert nurses can recognize when a newborn child is developing a life-threatening disease even before the child's blood tests come back positive. If you were to ask these nurses how they knew that the baby was getting seriously ill, they wouldn't be able to tell you specifically; many would simply attribute it to intuition. However, when researchers analyzed in detail what information the expert nurses paid attention to, they identified several cues and patterns about the baby's medical condition, some of which were not even part of the educational curriculum in nursing. In fact, some of the medical indicators these nurses tuned into were the opposite of what would be expected in sick adults.[9]

Similar to these nurses, Scott was an expert in his field. He had worked in his father's HR consulting firm for twelve years, and he knew the industry inside and out. When he saw the new software at the pitch meeting, his brain was processing more information than he was aware of. And when all the right cues were present, Scott's brain made an automatic decision—he needed to pivot his business and get behind this software start-up.

The realization that much of your behavior is habitual, automatic, and occurs without your conscious awareness is not easy to accept; indeed, it may seem *unbearable.* Although you might initially find comfort in blaming habits for your bad behaviors, this notion also raises questions about the meaning of life, morality, and personal responsibility. The celebrated Czech-born writer Milan Kundera explored this paradox in his novel *The Unbearable Lightness of Being,* which inspired the title of the *American Psychologist* article I mentioned earlier.[10] I'll leave it to him and the philosophers to contemplate the ontological implications of habits and the automaticity of human behavior.

As for Scott and everyone else, habits are not only bearable but *beneficial.* In fact, you would struggle to get anything done without them. Most likely you wouldn't even get out of the house in the morning if you had to make fresh decisions about every aspect of your daily routine: Should you have drip coffee, espresso, or cappuccino? Should you make it at home or buy it on your way to work? Should you brush your teeth before taking a shower? Should you shower or take a bath? Should you wash your hair before soaping up your body? What should you eat for breakfast? Bacon and eggs? Cereal with milk? Which brand of cereal? Cup of fruit? You get the idea—turning the elements of this routine into habits makes your life much easier, and more efficient.

If the fact that habits drive much of your daily behavior still gives you pause, remember this: conscious thought requires effort and energy, both limited resources. Your brain can only consciously process 110 bits of information per second, which in the grand scheme of things isn't much bandwidth. If it wasn't for automaticity and habits, that 110 bits per second would be all the information you could process, and your life would most likely resemble that of an animal driven by basic biological needs. Habits save you mental effort and allow you to achieve more at work and in life.

Great Leaders Hold Great Habits

When you think of your habits, the ones that most readily come to mind are usually the obvious ones, like your morning routine. But remember that close to half of your behavior is habitual, if not more, and that applies to your work as much as it does to what you do before you arrive at the office. How you start your workday, conduct meetings, respond to emails, answer the phone, and interact with coworkers are all to some degree driven by habits—some positive and others negative.

If you want a promotion, like Laura, or to make the right strategic decision for your business, like Scott, you need to have the right habits.

But how do you build those habits in the first place? Is it genetics? An MBA from a prestigious business school? Attending a leadership development program? Hiring an expensive executive coach? Having the right set of work and life experiences? Practicing every day?

Early leadership theorists postulated that leaders were born. These theorists were convinced that some people were genetically gifted with special characteristics that made them more likely to end up in leadership positions. However, twin studies have disproved this notion. When researchers examined the likelihood of fraternal and identical twins occupying a leadership role, they found that genetic factors accounted for only 30 percent.[11] The other 70 percent was not genetic but learned.

If leadership is mostly learned, then it stands to reason that people who end up in leadership roles must possess certain skills that others don't have. And this is indeed the case: Decades of research studies have thoroughly documented the skills of effective leaders. We know that the best leaders are good at influencing others, they communicate clearly, they plan ahead and think strategically, they delegate well—and that's just scratching the surface.

For example, researchers at Griffith University in Australia found that among the fifty-six luxury hotels they studied, managers who had a concrete vision, appealed to employees' values, empowered employees to make decisions, and coached and mentored them achieved better financial performance than those who did not.[12] Similarly, in a study of one hundred branch managers working at an industrial distribution company, managers who went beyond their own self-interest, demonstrated confidence, emphasized shared vision, motivated and inspired employees, encouraged innovation and creativity, and coached and mentored individual employees achieved higher year-over-year sales and profit margins.[13] The literature on the subject is prolific.

In my own research, my team and I reviewed the prolific literature on the subject to see if we could identify which skills are most common among effective leaders. After long hours of deliberation, we came up with a list of twenty-two core skills (see Figure 1-1), which became the organizing framework for the development of the Leader Habit Formula, as I will describe in detail in the next chapter.

Figure 1-1: Core Leadership Skills

GETTING THINGS DONE	FOCUSING ON PEOPLE
Planning & Execution Manage Priorities • Plan and Organize Work • Delegate Well • Create Urgency	***Persuasion & Influence*** Influence Others • Overcome Individual Resistance • Negotiate Well
Solving Problems & Making Decisions Analyze Information • Think Through Solutions • Make Good Decisions • Focus on Customers	***Growing People & Teams*** Empower Others • Mentor and Coach • Build Team Spirit
Leading Change Sell the Vision • Innovate • Manage Risk	***Interpersonal Skills*** Build Relationships • Show Caring • Listen Actively • Communicate Clearly • Speak with Charisma

At this point, it should be clear that the question at the heart of leadership development isn't, "Who has the ability to be a great leader?" but, "What's the best way to develop great leaders?"

If you've digested the key message in this chapter, you already know the answer: The best way to develop great leaders is to help people internalize the twenty-two core leadership skills to the point of automaticity—in other words, to turn those skills into habits. How do we do this?

In Figure 1-2, you can see how people build leadership skills. Let's put the amount of *practice* on the horizontal (x) axis and let's plot *automaticity* on the vertical (y) axis. With no practice whatsoever, you would be located on the left of the graph. With each day you practice, you would move slightly to the right. Remember that automaticity is the degree to which a task is processed without you having to pay close attention to its every detail—the degree to which the task happens automatically, without your conscious awareness. A new task requires practice before it starts to become automatic; the more you practice, the more automatic the task becomes—the higher the task's automaticity.

Figure 1-2: How People Build Skills

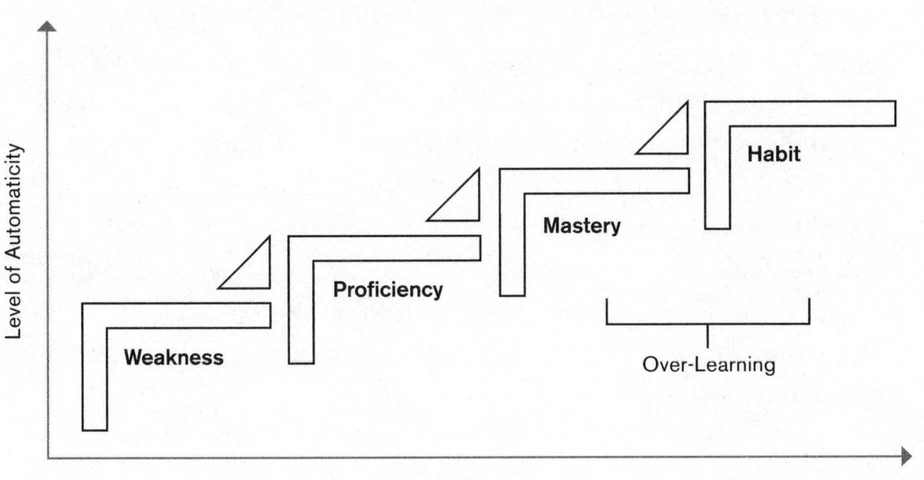

Any leadership skill starts as a *weakness*; you haven't practiced the skill and so you have to pay very close attention to it, because you don't yet know how to do it well. This stage takes a lot of effort and concentration, and you will make many mistakes along the way. Consider, for example, learning how to inspire your followers with a vision. There are multiple parts to this skill—being able to picture the arrival point, so that you can concretely define it for your followers (think "man on the moon"); having the foresight to understand where the group or company is heading; and understanding your followers' values and needs, so that your vision will appeal to them.

As you continue to practice the skill, your brain will start to automate some of the basic processes, like remembering the sequence of tasks and perhaps becoming better at a particular portion of the sequence. Maybe you will find a way to read your followers that enables you to quickly understand their values and needs without much concentration, or maybe you are a visual person who can easily imagine the arrival point. As your brain internalizes the processes that make up the different parts of the skill, the skill will begin to seem easier. You are now becoming *proficient.*

The more you continue to practice, especially the things you find more challenging, the closer you are getting to *mastery.* When you achieve mastery, you are now good at the skill, you can do it confidently, and others recognize your mastery. But even though you have mastered the skill, performing it still requires concentration and effort, because automaticity has not fully formed—the skill is not yet a habit. It takes practice *beyond* mastery, what psychologists refer to as over-learning, to fully form a habit. If you persist to the point of habit with the skill of inspiring followers with a vision, you will find that what once felt difficult and unnatural and required a lot of effort and concentration now happens effortlessly.

Where Did We Go Wrong with Leadership Development?

Most of us seem to intuitively understand the connection between leadership and success, because collectively we invest a lot of time and money in self-help classes and books intended to improve our leadership skills. In 2011, the self-help market in the United States was worth a whopping $10 billion. Although a significant portion of this money goes to health, fitness, and weight-loss programs, these are closely followed by financial, business, and personal development products.[14]

Likewise, businesses also invest heavily in leadership development. In 2012, American corporations spent $13.6 billion on leadership-development programs, an increase of 14 percent over the year before.

On average, companies were willing to spend thousands of dollars on training and resources for individual frontline and midlevel managers, more than $6,000 on senior executives, and upwards of $7,000 on high-potential employees.[15]

In fact, annual spending on leadership development has been steadily increasing since 1996. But there's a problem: All this investment isn't making us better leaders. On the contrary, there is a *negative* correlation between the macroeconomic amount spent on leadership development and our collective confidence in leadership.[16] In 2015, Brandon Hall Group surveyed more than five hundred organizations across thirty-four countries and thirty-one industries, and what they found was alarming: Half of the respondents reported that their current leaders didn't have the requisite skills to effectively lead their organizations at that time. Moreover, 71 percent of the organizations said their leaders were not prepared to lead the company in the future.[17]

Clearly there is a global leadership problem, despite people's desire to be better leaders, and despite the ever-increasing amount of money being spent on leadership development. Where are we going wrong?

As we've already seen, the problem isn't a lack of knowledge about the nature of leadership; conceptually, the skills and behaviors of great leaders are well understood. It turns out the problem is with the way most people approach leadership development.

"Read a Book or Take a Class"

If you want to learn a new skill or get better at something, the advice you're most likely to get from friends, family, colleagues, and mentors is "read a book or take a class." This is especially true in most corporations, where Human Resources will point you to a corporate university catalogue filled with online or in-person courses. In fact, training is the go-to solution for most personnel development in the business world. A

2017 LinkedIn survey found that 78 percent of companies use mainly instructor-led classes to teach what they consider the most important professional skills—leadership and people management.[18]

We regard books and classes as the ultimate way to learn because they often seem to be the easiest solutions, and because they're the most familiar. We spent most of our childhood and young adulthood learning in classrooms and reading from textbooks, so it's only natural that we continue to rely on them. But that's actually the problem: It turns out that books and classes aren't the best way to learn new skills. In fact, research in business settings shows that classroom-based training is usually not effective; estimates say that people end up using only 10 percent of what they learn in the classroom on the job.[19]

There are a number of reasons why traditional classroom and book-learning approaches to leadership development aren't effective. One is simply that we forget most of what we read about or are taught in the classroom.

In the early days of psychology, Hermann Ebbinghaus, a German scientist, tested the capacity of human memory by experimenting on himself. He set about learning nonsense words that followed a simple pattern of consonant-vowel-consonant, such as "REH," but had no meaning. Since the words were meaningless, he could not associate them with anything already stored in his memory. He dedicated time to studying his nonsense words over and over again, then tested his ability to remember them. In this way, he hoped to measure memory in its purest form.

Ebbinghaus found that one hour after studying the nonsense words, he had already forgotten 35 percent of them. After one day, he could remember only half of the words. And six days later, he had forgotten a staggering 85 percent of the nonsense words. This finding became known as Ebbinghaus's forgetting curve.[20] A similar pattern of forgetting has also been found among people who studied a foreign language, so it's not just nonsense words that we forget so rapidly.[21]

The second reason why traditional leadership development is ineffective is that, during training, people acquire mainly knowledge, not skills. Knowledge can be useful, if you can retain it and recall it at the right moments, but skills are what make us better at actually *doing* things, and skills are only developed through a systematic exercise regime known as *deliberate practice*, which is very different from acquiring conceptual knowledge.

Perhaps the best way to understand the difference between knowledge and skill is to look at music education. If you've ever learned how to play a musical instrument, such as piano, you know that simply taking a music theory class or watching a YouTube video of someone else playing the piano won't make you a concert pianist. To learn the many skills that are necessary to play the piano, you have to sit down at the keyboard yourself and practice those skills . . . a lot.

Learning to be a leader works the same way. Like playing the piano, leadership is more about skills than knowledge. The only way to become a better leader is to improve your leadership skills through deliberate, sustained practice—something traditional leadership training rarely provides.

The last and perhaps most important reason why traditional leadership training doesn't work is that it fails to take into account the overwhelming influence that habits have on human behavior. Most leadership training rests on the assumption that our daily behavior is rational, deliberate, and consciously controlled—but, as we have seen, this assumption couldn't be further from the truth. We are creatures of habit, personally and professionally, and no amount of classroom instruction or book learning alone can build the habits that will make us better leaders.

That's where the Leader Habit Formula comes in. By turning leadership skills into habits, we train ourselves to automatically respond to situations with effective behaviors, thus becoming more effective leaders.

This book is a guide to help you use the Leader Habit Formula to develop your leadership skills and turn them into habits. In the next chapter, you will learn how habits are formed, and I will describe the

Formula in detail, as well as the research behind it. In Part II, you will learn how to sustain the deliberate practice necessary to form habits; how simple, 5-minute exercises can become full-blown skills; and how to build your own customized Leader Habit workout using the Formula's catalogue of leadership skills and daily exercises, which is included in Part III. Finally, Part IV is intended for those responsible for helping other people develop leadership skills—parents, teachers, coaches, consultants, executive and life coaches, corporate managers, and human resources and organizational development professionals. It provides guidance for implementing the Formula in a variety of informal one-on-one and team contexts, and as part of formal leadership development programs.

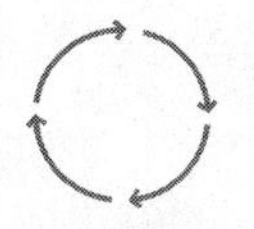

CHAPTER 2

The Leader Habit Formula

Saturday, July 6, 2013, was an unusually clear morning at San Francisco International Airport as Asiana Airlines Flight 214 prepared for final approach to runway 28L. With no clouds or fog over the bay, conditions were favorable for a routine landing. In the passenger cabin the seat belt sign went on, and everyone aboard felt a sense of relief that the eleven-hour flight would soon be over.

Lee Yoon-hye, an eighteen-year veteran with the airline, was the flight's cabin manager that day. As the Boeing 777 began its descent, she and the other flight attendants performed their final walkthrough of the cabin, collecting used cups and other trash, lifting window shades, and checking that passengers had fastened their seat belts. After the walkthrough was complete, Lee took her seat, buckled herself in, and waited for touchdown.

What happened next was anything but routine. The airliner came in too low and crash-landed when its main landing gear and tail hit a seawall at the end of the runway. The landing gear, tail section, and engines were ripped off during the crash. The main fuselage slid along the ground for 2,400 feet before stopping. "It was not the landing we usually do," Lee later said at a press conference. "We bumped hard, bumped again, leaned to both sides and stopped."[1] Within a minute, the wreckage caught fire and was engulfed in dark smoke.

As soon as Lee heard "emergency escape," her brain went into autopilot. There was no time to think, no time to plan, but she knew exactly what to do next. "I wasn't really thinking, but my body started carrying out the steps needed for an evacuation," Lee said later to a reporter. "When there was a fire, I was just thinking to extinguish it, not thinking that it's too dangerous or 'What am I going to do?'"

Lee's actions in the aftermath of the crash were the result of years of training. She was able to evacuate passengers, extinguish fires, and help the injured without consciously thinking about her actions because she had practiced these emergency procedures countless times, to the point that they had become ingrained as habits. When the emergency happened, the habits formed by her training took over and she responded automatically to the disaster's cues.

Clearly Lee's training was effective. Thanks in part to her automatic, habit-driven actions that day, all but two of the 307 passengers on board Flight 214 were rescued from the scene of the crash.

Lee's emergency-escape training worked because it was designed to instill habits—it focused on associating a specific cue (for example, fire) with a specific behavior (extinguish the fire) over and over again through deliberate practice until the behavior became an automatic response to the cue. Once this happened—once the trained behaviors became habits—Lee could respond to the cues of an emergency-escape situation without conscious effort. It didn't matter if she felt stressed or tired, or if she was in the middle of a life-threatening disaster; it didn't even matter if she was thinking about something else entirely. Whenever a cue presented itself, she would respond automatically with the specific behavior she had learned to pair with it, such as: fire (cue)—extinguish the fire (behavior). In the chaos that followed the crash of Flight 214, Lee's trained habits, and the similar habits of her fellow crew members, undoubtedly saved lives.

Lee Yoon-hye's actions are an example of how powerful habits can be when we train ourselves to automatically perform the right actions in response to particular cues. The principles of habit formation that prepared Lee to respond to an emergency escape are universal. The Leader Habit Formula takes these principles as a starting point and uses them to make leadership development simpler, more accessible, and more effective. (Remember that, at its core, leadership is nothing more than a set of habits.) The same way that Lee acquired her emergency-escape habits, you can develop the habits that will make you a better leader—if you know which key behaviors to focus on.

But first you need to understand how people form habits, how the Leader Habit Formula was developed, and how the basics of the Formula work.

Habit Formation

As you will recall from Chapter 1, a habit, whether good or bad, is simply an automatic response to a cue. We all have habits, and most aren't as dramatic as the ones Lee Yoon-hye learned in her emergency training. For example, sitting down with a cup of coffee may cue a smoker to light up a cigarette. Walking up to the bar may trigger an alcoholic to order a neat whiskey. Driving past a Starbucks may prompt a struggling dieter to stop for a Venti White Chocolate Crème Frappuccino. Once developed, habits are strong and hard to break, as many recovering smokers, alcoholics, and struggling dieters would attest.

All habits involve the pairing of a cue and a behavior: when the cue presents itself, you respond with the behavior. For example, let's say that you just moved to a new house, and since the move you've been having trouble finding your keys because you always put them in a different place when you come in the door. Frustrated, you decide to teach yourself to always put your keys in the same place. So today, after entering your new house (cue), you put your keys on the kitchen counter (behavior). You repeat the same thing tomorrow, and again the next day, and the day after that, and so on. Eventually, this pairing—entering your new house and placing your keys on the kitchen counter—becomes so ingrained that you perform the behavior automatically every time you enter the house; you don't even think about it. You have rehearsed the same behavior in response to the same cue over and over again, until it has turned into a habit. And now you always know where you put your keys!

The intentional repetition in this example is important. Habits are most effectively formed by repeatedly pairing the same cue with the same behavior through *deliberate practice*. A single response to a cue won't turn a behavior into a habit; it takes a lot of repetitions. This means that habit formation requires a lot of initial effort, even though the cue-behavior pairing that drives the process is simple.

Think back to when you first got in the habit of using a seat belt. How long did it take you to remember to always buckle up after getting in a car? Initially, it probably required a lot of mental effort—you probably had to rely on many reminders from parents and friends, or from the car's seat-belt warning chime, and it probably felt uncomfortable. But as more deliberate practice took place, the behavior became more comfortable and easier to perform, until finally it became a habit. It's the consistency of practice—the same cue paired with the same behavior over and over again—that results in the formation of a habit.[2]

In scientific terms, we call the state where a behavior occurs automatically in response to a cue without conscious thought *automaticity*. When a behavior achieves automaticity and becomes a habit, it is no longer deliberate or consciously controlled. The smoker lights up a cigarette automatically after sitting down with a cup of coffee; she only realizes that she's smoking after seeing the lit cigarette. The alcoholic asks for a neat whiskey automatically after hearing "What are you drinking?"; he doesn't even think about other beverages. The struggling dieter automatically heads for the drive-through after seeing a Starbucks sign; she doesn't consider the 510 calories in the Venti White Chocolate Crème Frappuccino. Lee Yoon-hye hears "emergency escape" and springs into action, saving lives; she doesn't stop to worry about what caused the plane to crash or how dangerous the situation is.

Automaticity kicks in after you practice a behavior beyond mastery—that is, continuing to practice even after you think you can't get any better. Scientists have found that when you start a new behavior, your brain forms a mental model of it. As you practice your new behavior, your brain works hard to update its mental model to better predict patterns of that behavior and to overcome obstacles that may prevent the behavior from occurring. Over time, and with enough repetition, your brain refines its mental model to make the behavior more efficient by cutting out unnecessary processes and eliminating energy waste. We aren't consciously aware that our brain is doing this, but the results can be measured in the laboratory. In fact, researchers have found that the greatest energy and effort reductions occur during practice that happens *after* a skill has already been mastered.[3] This period of deliberate practice after mastery is referred to as *over-learning*. This is when automaticity happens and habits are formed.

How does over-learning fit with our examples of the smoker and the alcoholic? You might point out that people don't deliberately practice smoking and drinking behaviors in order to form these habits, and you would be right. We can all think of habits we have formed without intending to, and without deliberate practice. That's because the repetition of a cue-behavior pairing is only part of the story. The other part is *reward*.

In 1947, renowned American psychologist B. F. Skinner observed something extraordinary. He had been doing experiments with pigeons for several years and had succeeded in teaching them how to ask for food by performing various tasks. In one of his simpler experiments, Skinner took a group of pigeons and placed each one in a separate cage fitted with an automatic feeding machine. The pellet dispenser was set up to feed the pigeons for a few minutes each day at predetermined, regular time intervals. For example, from 3:50 to 4:00 p.m. each day, the pigeon would receive food pellets exactly one minute apart, and then the feeding would stop until the following day.

As the experiment progressed, Skinner noticed that some of the pigeons began developing bizarre habits. One bird would start turning its body around anti-clockwise three times in anticipation of food. Another one would move its head side to side resembling a swinging pendulum. There were many other examples of odd behavior, and by the end of the experiment, three-quarters of the birds had developed strange habits. Skinner realized that the pigeons had developed these habits randomly: whatever behavior they happened to be performing during the feeding time was rewarded by the food pellets. Because of the reward, the pigeons learned to associate that particular behavior with the food pellet, and so they repeated the behavior over and over again in anticipation of food, until that behavior turned into a habit.[4]

Skinner's experiment demonstrated that a reward is the second condition necessary for habit formation. Simply put, behaviors that are repeatedly rewarded turn into habits. This explains how people develop habitual behaviors related to smoking, alcohol, and food. The pleasure people receive from chemicals contained in cigarette smoke, alcohol, and fatty or sugary foods is the reward that drives them to repeat those behaviors again and again. When the rewarded behaviors are practiced in the presence of the same cue enough times, the full habit cycle is born: *cue–behavior–reward.*

It doesn't matter whether you begin the habit cycle with the cue-behavior pairing or the behavior-reward pairing. The important thing to remember is that both a cue and a reward need to be present for a behavior to turn into a habit. On the one hand, you can start by deliberately practicing a behavior in response to a cue, as Lee Yoon-hye did for years during her flight attendant training. On the other hand, if you derive satisfaction (reward) from performing a behavior, the reward will motivate you to continue practicing beyond the point of mastery. Either way, once you reach over-learning, your brain refines its mental model, automaticity kicks in, and now you have formed a new habit.

The *cue–behavior–reward* cycle explains how habits are formed. At a high level, the process seems simple, but there are some details that we need to explore further. For example, you've probably noticed that some behaviors easily turn into habits (smoking, drinking, eating unhealthy foods, to name just a few), while others require more effort to establish (eating healthy, exercising regularly). We know that the habit cycle is the same for all behaviors, so what accounts for the differences in effort, and how can we identify the characteristics that cause certain behaviors to become habits faster than others?

Accelerating Habit Formation: Simple, Individual, and Consistent Behaviors

An ultrasonic burst of sound pings the deep black waters of the Atlantic Ocean. You soon identify the source: an enemy submarine roughly ten miles away. Your task? Avoid combat and bring your submarine and crew intact to a military port on the other side of the Atlantic Ocean. You must navigate your submarine through underwater obstacles, maintain speed, temperature, and oxygen levels, ready the torpedoes, monitor the sonar, and raise the shields.

Thankfully, this is just a computer game and you are a participant in an experiment on the effectiveness of different training methods. Crossing the Atlantic Ocean in a submarine is a very complex task, for which you received training earlier that day. For your group, the researchers broke down the entire transatlantic journey into smaller subtasks, or chunks, and you only practiced one small chunk at a time. Once you mastered that one small chunk of the trip, you moved on to practicing the next leg of the long journey.

Participants in the other research group were trained differently: They didn't break down the trip into smaller chunks. Instead, they practiced the entire transatlantic voyage from beginning to end as a single, complex task.

Which group learned faster? Your group did, because it focused on practicing one small chunk at a time. Those who practiced the entire complex task took longer to learn.[5]

The research findings are clear: *Simple* behaviors are more likely to become habits than complex ones.[6] This doesn't mean you can't turn complex behaviors into habits; it means you will have more success if you first break down a complex behavior into smaller behaviors—a process psychologists call *chunking*. You already have experience doing this. Think back to how you learned to walk, play a musical instrument, or master a sport. Each activity involves many complex behaviors that would be impossible to learn all at once. Instead, you practiced one chunk at a time—you took your first step as a baby, you learned the first section of a musical piece, you learned to dribble before learning to shoot. Only after you mastered one chunk did you move on to practicing the next.

Another characteristic of behaviors that turn into habits faster is that they are *individual*. This means having only one behavior associated with a particular cue. If you try to practice multiple behaviors in response to the same cue, the behaviors will compete with each other and your brain will not know which to prioritize. This makes it harder for the brain to refine its behavior models, and can prevent automaticity from taking place. Research suggests that having multiple behaviors in direct response to the same cue can actually lessen your chances that any one behavior will become a habit.[7] (This is another reason to break down complex skills into simple chunks. Chunking makes it easier to be sure that you are pairing each simple behavior with its own unique cue.)

Finally, behaviors that are *consistent* become habits faster. This makes sense if you remember that your brain is building and refining a model for each behavior that you practice. A behavior that is always the same is easier to model—and its model is easier to refine—than one that is always performed differently. For example, let's say that you want to become better at empowering others, and the behavior you are trying to turn into a habit is asking your direct reports which decisions they are comfortable making. The more consistent you can keep the question you ask, the faster the habit will form. But imagine if you were to phrase the question several different ways, sometimes, "What decisions related to this assignment are you comfortable making?" and other times, "How can we give you more control over the project?" The more variations you introduce, the more work your brain has to do to account for them. The result is that it will take a lot longer for the behavior to achieve automaticity.

The trifecta of *simple, individual,* and *consistent* is the key to understanding which behaviors have the highest potential to quickly become habits. It was also my inspiration for the Leader Habit Formula.

As you will recall, there are twenty-two core leadership skills, and each one is complex and difficult to master. This is one of the reasons that conventional approaches to leadership development have proven so ineffective—trying to learn twenty-two complex skills all at once is like rehearsing an entire transatlantic submarine voyage from start to finish. It might be theoretically possible to master everything, but in practice it almost never works. There are too many behaviors competing for attention. In the end, few of them, if any, stick.

But, with the trifecta in mind, I realized that it was possible to break down the complex leadership skills into smaller micro-behaviors. Once I had identified all the micro-behaviors, I could use them as the basis for simple, focused exercises that anyone could easily practice on a daily basis to build the habits that would, over time, add up to improved leadership skills. The idea promised a new, more effective approach to leadership development—if the complex skills could indeed be broken down into smaller micro-behaviors.

Leadership Skills, Deconstructed

The agenda for my research team was set: We would study the twenty-two most common leadership skills and attempt to catalogue the micro-behaviors that make up each skill by observing and analyzing the behavior of almost eight hundred leaders from around the world. As you might expect, this was not an easy task.

Our biggest challenge was finding a *standardized* situation that would allow us to observe such a large number of leaders in action. By standardized, I mean a situation that was exactly the same for every leader—the same company, the same job title, the same leadership scenarios encountered in exactly the same order.

Why did we care so much about standardization? Because only by keeping all of the situational details constant could we tease out the differences in the participants' leadership behaviors and make meaningful comparisons between effective and ineffective leaders.

We decided to use a *live leadership simulation* for the standardized scenario. We built a realistic, 3-hours-in-the-life simulation that could be delivered virtually and included live role-plays with human actors—think of it as an elaborate Harvard Business School case study come to life. Before participating in the simulation, the participants received pre-work documents to study. They learned about their fictitious new organization and their fictitious new job—the organizational chart, financial statements, strategic plan, industry trends, and the like. The simulation started with a few emails waiting for them to address and a schedule with meetings. We trained actors to play different roles, like an underperforming employee who needed guidance, an obnoxious TV reporter, and the chief operating officer of the company. The actors connected with the participants via webcam and engaged them in short role-plays. In between the role-plays, participants received more emails that presented them with different problems to solve.

We recorded every role-play interaction and every email exchange and asked independent assessors to observe the leaders' behaviors in those recordings. Our assessors had at least a master's degree in psychology or a related field, and had completed extensive training on how to properly observe and code various leadership behaviors. Each participant was observed by at least three independent assessors, and we averaged the assessors' ratings to increase objectivity.

Over the course of several years, my research team collected observations of 795 leaders, of which 56 percent were men. The leaders in our sample held senior executive (26 percent), midlevel leadership (27 percent), and frontline manager (23 percent) positions. Their average age was forty years, and they had on average eight years of management experience. Most leaders identified as Caucasian/White/European (48 percent), 30 percent as Latino/Hispanic, 4 percent as Asian/Pacific Islander, and 2 percent as Black/African. Forty-four percent were located in North America, 29 percent in Europe or Africa, 22 percent in South America, and 5 percent in Asia-Pacific. Just under half of the leaders we studied held a postgraduate degree (49 percent), and an additional 33 percent held an undergraduate degree. They worked in virtually every industry, including manufacturing (23 percent), health care (12 percent), education services (10 percent), construction (8 percent), financial services (7 percent), and professional services (7 percent).

After compiling all assessor observations, we performed statistical analyses of 159 different micro-behaviors. We examined how often each micro-behavior occurred, whether it was categorized under the correct leadership skill and related to the other relevant micro-behaviors, whether it predicted successful performance of the leader, and whether our assessors agreed on the micro-behavior's effectiveness. Through these statistical analyses, we eliminated eighty micro-behaviors that didn't meet predetermined thresholds for all of these criteria. We were left with seventy-nine micro-behaviors that constitute the twenty-two core leadership skills.

With our catalogue of micro-behaviors complete, the next step in developing the Leader Habit Formula was to create simple exercises for the micro-behaviors that would enable anyone to easily turn them into habits. The habit cycle dictated that the exercises needed to pair each micro-behavior with both a cue and a reward, and in order for the exercise to most effectively form a habit, each micro-behavior would have to be paired with a natural cue. This meant that we would have to be careful in selecting our cue-behavior pairings. Fortunately, research has identified the characteristics that make some cues better than others.

Effective Behavioral Cues

You've probably been to the cinema with someone that digs through an entire bucket of popcorn before the movie is over. No doubt this person enjoys the taste, but chances are his or her popcorn-eating at the movies is more the result of a habit than a genuine love of the salty snack food. Have you seen this person also buy popcorn at the gas station or eat it at a Christmas party? Probably not. The fact is, most people who eat popcorn at the movies do so because they are at the movies.

Researchers at Duke University designed an experiment to test whether movie-goers ate popcorn at the theater because of a conscious desire for popcorn or purely out of habit. They reasoned that fresh popcorn tastes much better than seven-day-old, stale popcorn (of course it does). If participants ate the same amount of stale popcorn as fresh popcorn when they were at the movie theater, then they must be eating out of habit and not because the stale popcorn tastes good. The researchers invited two groups of students to preview trailers for upcoming films in a movie theater. One group was served fresh popcorn, and the other group received the seven-day-old, stale popcorn. When the students left, the researchers weighed the remaining buckets of popcorn to see how much the students had consumed. The results showed that the students ate the same amount of popcorn regardless of whether it was stale or fresh.[8] Indeed, moviegoers eat popcorn out of habit, not because it tastes good.

But what if you changed the setting? Would students still eat as much of the bad-tasting, stale popcorn? The researchers changed the setting in a follow-up experiment to a campus meeting room. Instead of previewing trailers, the students viewed music videos. Would this different environment still trigger the habitual eaters to eat the stale popcorn? The answer is no. Students ate much less of the stale popcorn (similar to nonhabitual eaters) when the setting changed from a movie theater to a campus meeting room.

A movie theater is itself a strong, *natural* cue to eat popcorn. The darkened room, the cinema seats, and the big screen all serve as organic triggers to remind us to eat popcorn. These cues are naturally embedded in the environment—they are present in the same context where the behavior occurs.[9]

Contrast this with an *artificial* cue, such as a reminder that you create—for example, a sticky note on your computer or an alarm on your phone. When people want to remember to do something, they usually set an artificial cue. Artificial cues can be useful in the beginning of habit formation, when you might need reminders to help sustain your practice, but they don't work as well in the long term. This fact shouldn't come as a surprise, given what you now know about habits being automatic behavioral responses to specific cues. If the cue paired with a behavior is not embedded in the same context as the behavior itself, then you can't count on that cue to trigger the behavior at the right time and in the right circumstances. What happens when the artificial cue goes away (the sticky note falls off your computer, you forget to set your alarm)? The new behavior goes away with it. Therefore, if you want to build a new habit, you must look for a naturally occurring, embedded cue to pair it with.

Imagine for a second that I asked you to go through my entire book and underline all references to a mammal or an object that can be moved. Now let's say that I asked your friend to also go through my entire book but instead underline the word "she." Who do you think will develop the habit faster—you or your friend? In an experiment at the University of Tromso in Norway, participants were asked to do exactly these tasks. One group underlined every occurrence of the word "she" in a body of text, while another group underlined every instance of a mammal or an object that can be moved in the same text. Not surprisingly, those who were underlining the specific word "she" developed the habit faster than those who were asked to look for every possible mammal or moveable object.[10]

Cues that are more difficult to spot do not lend themselves to automatic behaviors and are less likely to form habits. The cue "she" was *simple, concrete*, and *obvious*, while the cue "mammal or an object that can be moved" was vague, abstract, and complex. Remember that your brain is trying to streamline its mental model of the cue-behavior pairing. If the cue is complex and difficult to spot, then your brain has to work harder to identify many variations of the cue, and the journey to automaticity and habit will take longer.

Thankfully, Lester Farnsworth Wire, a police officer in Salt Lake City, Utah, must have known that good cues should be obvious when he designed the first electric traffic light in 1912.[11] The colors green and red are opposite each other on the color wheel, which makes the contrast simple and obvious. Just imagine how many more accidents would occur if Wire had chosen orange to mean "go" and red to mean "stop." Because the contrast between red and green lights is readily obvious, your brain can easily associate the "go" behavior with a green light and "brake" behavior with a red light.

Similarly, a good cue must be *unique*—it shouldn't be already associated with other behaviors.[12] This is just another way of expressing the *individual* characteristic described earlier, which stated that behaviors more quickly become habits when only one behavior is paired with a given cue. So, on the flip side, if you're looking for a cue to pair with a new behavior, don't choose one that is already paired with another habit. In this case, you can actually use the end of an existing habit as a cue to the new behavior (I will discuss how you can create a chain of behaviors in Chapter 4).

So what makes a good cue? A good cue should be naturally embedded in the same context where you want the behavior to happen; it has to be simple, concrete, and obvious; and it has to be unique. Fortunately, there is one particular type of a cue that meets all these criteria and significantly speeds up the habit-building process. That cue is the end of a specific event or task.[13] Here are some examples: after you start your computer in the morning; after you finish breakfast; after you finish lunch; after you finish reading an email; after you make coffee; after you pick up the phone; after you realize that you need to make a decision; after you finish a meeting; after you greet a colleague . . . you get the idea.

The Leader Habit Formula is grounded in event-based cues. When creating the 5-minute exercises for the leadership micro-behaviors, my research team identified the tasks and events that tend to naturally precede each behavior. Choosing from these natural cues, we made sure each cue-behavior pairing was unique whenever possible. An additional benefit of using only natural, event-based cues for the pairings is that all the exercises share the same format: after an event or task finishes, you do the micro-behavior. It's simple and easy to remember.

Of course, even with the simple exercises and unique cues the Leader Habit Formula provides, you know that the only way to turn your desired leadership micro-behaviors into habits is through deliberate practice. So, naturally, you're wondering—how much practice is it going to take?

Practice, Practice, Practice

"May all your troubles last as long as your New Year's resolutions," is perhaps my favorite Joey Adams quote. We've all tried to start a new habit in the beginning of the year, weight loss being one of the more popular aspirations. In fact, more than 45 million Americans make a resolution to lose weight every year. The result is over $60 billion spent annually on gym memberships, weight-loss books, and workout videos.[14] But few people manage to turn their fitness and weight-loss resolutions into habits: on average, by the second week of February, 80 percent of new gym memberships drop off.[15]

There are many reasons why most New Year's resolutions fail; one is that people just don't practice long enough for a habit to form.

Popular claims say that it takes twenty-one days to develop a new habit. This is based on Dr. Maxwell Maltz's 1960 claim that it takes "a minimum of 21 days" for people to adjust to a change from surgery, like cosmetic surgery or amputation.[16] However, getting used to your new look is quite different from developing a jogging habit.

So how long does it really take for a behavior to become a habit?

Research shows that the answer is over three times what popular claims suggest: *an average of sixty-six days.*[17] In this research study, college students chose a healthy eating, drinking, or exercise behavior they wanted to turn into a habit. The students had some freedom to choose their behavior as long as it wasn't something they already did, it was simple enough, and they picked a salient cue to trigger the behavior. Some examples included eating a piece of fruit or drinking a glass of water with lunch. Others chose to run for fifteen minutes before dinner. Each day, the students logged whether they had performed the behavior and whether they had to think about doing the behavior. It took an average of sixty-six days for the students to start doing their behavior automatically without thinking about it, and that's the number of days I recommend as the minimum practice for each Leader Habit exercise.

It is important to note that the sixty-six-day time frame is an average. Some people will form habits more quickly, while others take longer. Similarly, some habits will take longer to form than others, even when the behavior is simple, individual, and consistent and paired with a good cue. For these reasons it is better not to think in terms of a set time frame, but in terms of your desired behavior reaching automaticity. When this happens, the habit is formed, and not until then. It could take just a few days or forty-five days, or exactly sixty-six days, or it could take a hundred days. The exact amount of time it takes you to form a particular habit is not important, as long as you actually form the habit. What matters is that you understand the habit cycle and set your expectations accordingly. The Leader Habit Formula incorporates the sixty-six-day average as a baseline to guide your efforts and as a reminder that you need to practice a lot, and for a lot longer, than popular beliefs about habit formation suggest. Remember that automaticity only happens during over-learning—when you keep practicing after you have already mastered the new behavior. If you are unsure whether or not your habit is fully formed, go through the Automaticity Checklist in Figure 2-1.

Figure 2-1. Automaticity Checklist

Here is a way to check whether the behavior you are practicing has reached automaticity:

- ❑ Does the behavior occur consistently each time the cue is presented?
- ❑ Do you engage in this behavior without thinking or without having to remind yourself to do it?
- ❑ Have you realized that you were performing the behavior, but can't remember deliberately starting it?
- ❑ Does the behavior occur right away after you encounter the cue (i.e., within seconds)?
- ❑ Have you been practicing this behavior in response to the same cue for two to three months?
- ❑ Do you have to use purposeful effort to *stop* the behavior after being cued?
- ❑ Are you more efficient at completing the behavior today than when you started?

The more you answer "yes" to these questions, the closer you are to forming a habit. When in doubt, keep practicing.

Don't Forget the Reward

If you remember the story about the bizarre habits developed by the pigeons in the Skinner experiment I described earlier, then you have probably noticed by now that the Leader Habit Formula needs one last element to be complete: the reward.

As Skinner's pigeons demonstrated, the reward is a crucial component of the habit cycle. If the reward is strong enough, it will form a habit on its own. For example, opiate drugs like heroin provide several strong rewards: they lessen pain and anxiety, and initially produce a sudden feeling of warmth in the lower abdomen that resembles orgasm. During the Vietnam War, about half of U.S. soldiers tried opium or heroin, and 20 percent of them became regular users.[18] The reward opiates delivered was strong enough for these soldiers to form a habit. Although drugs are an extreme example, you would be correct to assume that some types of rewards are stronger than others, and that stronger rewards can speed up the formation of habits. In fact, there is a particular type of reward that works especially well with leadership habits, as you will see in a moment.

Researchers used a clever experiment with LEGO figures to study how people respond to different types of rewards. In this experiment, research participants were divided into two groups and asked to assemble LEGO figures for diminishing amounts of money. Participants received the most money for their first assembled LEGO figure and were paid less and less for each subsequent figure thereafter. In group one, each time someone completed a LEGO figure, the figure would be securely displayed under the table. But in group two, each time someone finished a LEGO figure, the researcher would immediately disassemble it in plain view of the participants. Both groups were offered the same amount of money for each assembled figure. Which group didn't value the rewards and gave up first?

It probably comes as no surprise that the second group stopped making LEGO figures long before the first group, despite the fact that the monetary reward was identical for both groups. What the experiment highlights is the importance of *intrinsic reward.*[19] Intrinsic rewards are stronger than extrinsic rewards because the latter quickly lose their value to people.

Extrinsic rewards are tangible, physical things that you receive for doing something—for example, a prize or a medal or a certificate. In the case of the LEGO experiment, the extrinsic reward was the money the participants received for each figure they assembled.

An intrinsic reward is something intangible, like a feeling of personal satisfaction or a sense of accomplishment. In the LEGO experiment, the participants whose figures were put on display received an intrinsic reward from having their work acknowledged. This intrinsic reward was more powerful than the extrinsic reward (the money), and it motivated the group that received it to work longer. For the second group, the extrinsic reward alone was not enough to keep them motivated. In the case of these two LEGO-building groups, and also in most other settings, people care more about intrinsic rewards.[20]

Selecting the wrong type of reward is where most habit-forming efforts fail. When people resolve to start working out or dieting, they tend to select an extrinsic reward—they pay themselves money, go on a vacation, or rely on praise and recognition from their friends. But as we saw in the LEGO experiment, those extrinsic rewards quickly lose value and people give up. In contrast, intrinsic rewards don't lose their value. This is what makes intrinsic rewards so effective as part of the habit cycle and why they are incorporated into the Leader Habit Formula.

The key to intrinsic reward is that you derive satisfaction from doing the behavior. You inherently want to do the behavior because it feels gratifying in and of itself. So how do you find an intrinsic reward to pair with the behavior you want to turn into a habit, especially in the context of building Leader Habits?

When it comes to finding leadership behaviors that will be intrinsically rewarding to you, you must start thinking of your everyday behaviors as expressions of your personality. If you are an extrovert, it is intrinsically rewarding for you to socialize with colleagues, because you get energy from people. But if you are an introvert, the opposite is true: social interactions drain energy from you; for an introvert, there is no intrinsic reward in communicating with others. Your personality determines which behaviors are intrinsically rewarding for you because it is inherently satisfying to act in ways that are consistent with your personality.

In 1977, researchers tested the notion that people would experience more satisfaction from jobs that allowed them to express their personality. With a personality questionnaire, they measured Navy personnel in ten different jobs on how ambitious they were. The ten jobs were categorized as "challenging" vs. "non-challenging" based on the amount of formal Navy training required to qualify for the job. Arguably, the more challenging the job, the more formal training it required. Examples of the challenging jobs included radar maintenance and parachute rigging; the non-challenging jobs included unskilled maintenance and storekeeping. Researchers then assessed the participants to determine who got more satisfaction from their jobs: ambitious people in challenging jobs, or ambitious people in non-challenging jobs.

The results of the experiment confirmed that people get more satisfaction from work that allows them to express their personality. Ambitious Navy personnel experienced less satisfaction in non-challenging jobs than when they held challenging jobs. [21] The challenging jobs offered more variety, opportunity to learn, and required many different skills. Ambitious people are competitive and motivated by achievement, and the challenging jobs spoke directly to their preferences. Ambitious participants derived intrinsic reward from the challenging jobs and so their overall satisfaction with their jobs was also higher.

Behaviors that are consistent with our personality are more likely to become habits because we naturally derive satisfaction from doing them. This is the power of intrinsic reward—*the reward is built into the behavior.* The Leader Habit Formula is designed to help you take advantage of intrinsic rewards: When you are deciding which micro-behaviors to develop into habits, it is best to choose the ones that are consistent with your personality (you will learn how to do this in Chapter 3).

Putting It All Together

Habits are powerful. Once a behavior becomes a habit, it happens automatically in response to its cue, without any conscious thought. The goal of the Leader Habit Formula is to help you harness this power to improve your leadership skills through a process that is effective, efficient, and easy to sustain. The Formula breaks down twenty-two core leadership skills into their constituent micro-behaviors and provides simple, focused exercises for each micro-behavior (see Part III for the complete catalogue of leadership skills, micro-behaviors, and Leader Habit exercises). These exercises can be completed in just five minutes of practice every day, and they are designed specifically to trigger habit formation. Each micro-behavior has been paired with a naturally occurring cue that is probably already part of your normal workday, and the Formula uses intrinsic reward to complete the habit cycle. After sixty-six days of deliberately practicing an exercise, you should find that the micro-behavior has become automatic—it has become a habit. Then you choose a new micro-behavior and repeat the process. The more Leader Habits you build through this process, the more your leadership skills will improve.

PART II

BUILD YOUR LEADERSHIP SKILLS

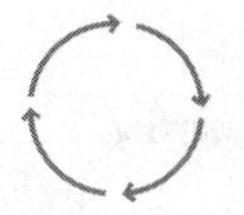

CHAPTER 3

How to Sustain Practice

To outward appearances, Tristan Pang seems like an ordinary fifteen-year-old boy from New Zealand. Like many of his friends, he goes to school and enjoys hobbies, such as playing the piano and swimming for the local club. But while his peers are still attending high school, Tristan is studying at Auckland College. In fact, he was reading fiction and nonfiction as well as working on high-school-level mathematics at the age of two, and by age eleven he had earned the highest grade possible on the Cambridge International A Level examinations (equivalent to U.S. high school senior year). That same year, Tristan became the youngest person in New Zealand to deliver a TEDxYouth talk.[1]

Tristan's extraordinary educational achievements are the result of an extraordinary amount of practice. While his peers followed the school curriculum from year to year, Tristan pushed himself beyond these artificially prescribed boundaries and continued to study independently. In mathematics, he picked up books on algebra, geometry, and statistics from Year 1 to Year 13 (the equivalent of spanning the primary and secondary education curriculum in the United States). Studying at home, he worked his way through all thirteen books on algebra before moving on to the next thirteen books on geometry, and so on.[2]

If you remember back to your childhood, you probably wanted to avoid studying as much as possible—and you certainly didn't want to spend your free time studying mathematics. What made Tristan want to study math so much, and where did he find the motivation?

Tristan revealed the secret behind his relentless study of subjects like math, physics, and chemistry in his TEDxYouth talk "Quest is fun, be nosey." For him, these subjects are not dry and boring; on the contrary, Tristan finds them fun and exciting. In fact, the more difficult the subject, the more satisfaction he got out of mastering it. "It's my passion and it's my nature, which is full of nosiness. From the very beginning, I had passion for all these subjects and I wanted to find out more." To Tristan, exploring scientific topics is "just like playing puzzles; it is challenging and fun . . . I normally work hour after hour without realizing the time flying by until my mom asks me to stop."[3]

For Tristan and many other gifted children, practicing the subjects that interest them comes naturally and is enjoyable. Their parents and teachers are not forcing them to practice, and these children are also not forcing practice on themselves; they derive so much satisfaction from the practice itself that they simply cannot stop.

Getting in the Flow

Psychologists refer to the state that Tristan experiences when practicing mathematics or physics as *flow*, a term first popularized by Mihály Csíkszentmihályi.[4] Flow, also commonly known as "being in the zone," is characterized by an experience of being so deeply involved in an activity you find intrinsically rewarding that you lose track of everything else. All distractions disappear; you don't feel hunger, boredom, or stress; you don't notice the passage of time; all your attention is focused on the task at hand. In his 2004 TED talk "Flow, the Secret to Happiness," Csíkszentmihályi described the experience as a state of intense focus that leads to "ecstasy" and "clarity," in which "you know exactly what you want to do from one moment to another."[5] In a related example, documentary director Ondi Timoner describes how she sometimes feels when editing her films: "It's a transcendent feeling, as if I have to race to physically manifest the ideas and connections that are flowing through me. I become a conduit as puzzle pieces fly into place."[6]

The concept of flow has appeared throughout human history and across cultures. In Japanese martial arts, for example, the word for this type of effortless vigilance is *zanshin*, which, literally translated, means "the mind with no remainder."[7] Or consider this vivid description from the 4th-century BC Chinese philosopher Zhuangzi in his account of a butcher at work cutting up an ox:

> At every touch of his hand, every heave of his shoulder, every move of his feet, every thrust of his knee—zip! zoop! He slithered the knife along with a zing, and all was in perfect rhythm, as though he were performing the dance of the Mulberry Grove or keeping time to the Jingshou music.[8]

More recently, in what has become foundational work in the field of positive psychology, Csíkszentmihályi and fellow researchers gathered journal entries and interviews from people who regularly experience flow.[9] From these accounts, a consistent narrative emerged: In addition to being unaware of distractions and the passage of time, people reported becoming so engrossed in their practice that the activity itself became effortless. People who regularly experienced flow noted that it led them deeper into their passion, helped them become more skilled and knowledgeable in their niche, and ultimately led to greater success in their careers. The same experience was reported by people with varied backgrounds and from many different disciplines, from motorcycle gang members to sheep herders, revealing that anyone can experience flow in the area of their passion.

Remember that last part: *Anyone can experience flow in the area of their passion*. Although it is possible to experience flow while performing mundane tasks, such as washing dishes or folding laundry, people most often achieve flow while pursuing something they enjoy. This feeling of enjoyment—an intrinsic reward—is one of the keys to achieving flow.

I'm not suggesting that you need to achieve flow while doing your 5-minute Leader Habit exercise each day, although it certainly is possible that you could reach a point where practicing a particular leadership skill that you enjoy *does* trigger a state of flow. If you get to that point, great; if not, don't worry. The important thing to understand is that flow is an extreme form of focused and deliberate practice, that it is made possible by the power of intrinsic rewards, and that you can harness that same power to help you sustain your own daily practice. Simply put: If you enjoy doing something, you're more likely to keep doing it. So, if you want to be successful at turning leadership skills into habits, you need to pick skills that you will enjoy practicing. That means identifying the skills that align with the behaviors you find intrinsically satisfying. And that means thinking of your behaviors as expressions of your personality.

It's Hard to Be Someone You're Not

In order to identify which leadership skills you will derive intrinsic satisfaction from practicing, you must first understand the concept of *personality traits*. At the heart of this concept is the age-old question: Do you act the same way in every situation, or do you change your behavior based on the environment and people around you?

Imagine that you are at a dinner party at your neighbors' house. They are a lesbian couple. Sam is tall and muscular, with a short haircut. She is dominant not only in her appearance but also in her speech. She controls the conversation, making it obvious which topics she wishes to discuss, and confidently states her opinions. Her wife, Cindy, on the contrary, is slim, blonde, sharply dressed, and outwardly feminine. Her demeanor is warm, pleasant, agreeable, and submissive. Both women are sitting across the table from you, and you engage them both in a casual dinner conversation. Does your behavior change depending on which one you are talking to? Do you become more submissive when talking to Sam and more dominant when talking to Cindy?

Researchers at the University of Helsinki in Finland created a clever experiment based on a similar scenario to study the extent to which people's behavior remains constant in different situations. They trained four actors to play very different roles: one acted dominantly, one was submissive, another warm, and the last one argumentative. The four actors were seated in separate rooms equipped with a video camera. The researchers sent students from room to room to discuss a random topic for five minutes, so that every student interacted with each actor. The interactions were recorded, and researchers later observed and scored the students' behaviors in the four different situations. Did the students become more dominant or submissive based on which actor they interacted with? Were they friendlier toward the warm actor than the argumentative one?

It turns out the students' behavior was largely consistent from one conversation to the next, regardless of which actor they were talking to. In fact, 42 percent of their behavior remained consistent and only 4 percent of the variation in their behavior was attributed to the different situations.[10] The remaining 54 percent of the students' behavior was random—that is to say, it was influenced by factors the researchers couldn't systematically explain within the context of their experiment. The conclusion we can draw from this study is that a large portion of people's behavior *is* consistent from situation to situation, but not to the point of being deterministic. The fact that over half of the observed behavior was random leaves plenty of room for conscious processing and free will. Because your personality influences your everyday behavior, you tend to act consistently from situation to situation. These consistent patterns of behavior are one source of intrinsic reward—it feels good to do things that feel natural to us.

The notion that a significant portion of our behavior remains consistent in different situations and around different people is central to the concept of personality traits. You can think of personality traits as stable patterns of behavior that define who you are: Some people are introverted, others are extroverted. Some are friendly, others argumentative. Some are organized, others scattered. Personality traits are genetically predisposed and stay largely unchanged throughout our lives. Often we're not aware of their powerful influence on us because, like habits, the patterns of behavior that arise from our personality traits are unconscious.

When we act according to our personality traits, our behavior feels natural and effortless. We can behave differently if we choose to—introverts can act like extroverts, agreeable people can start arguments—but going against our traits requires conscious effort and is difficult to sustain as you'll see demonstrated in the next research study.

At the University of Virginia, researchers studied what happens when people act contrary to their personality traits. In this experiment, the researchers assigned undergraduate students into two groups based on their personality—expressive and inexpressive. Those in the expressive group had traits that predisposed them to act in an animated, vivid, dramatic way. Those in the inexpressive group were predisposed to unemotional, flat behavior. These students were asked to state their opinion about a controversial subject on video, but with a twist: Expressive students were asked to act inhibited and inexpressive students were asked to be animated. A third group of students watched these videos and rated the expressiveness of their colleagues.

When the ratings were tallied up, the results showed that expressive students were always rated as more animated than inexpressive students, even when trying to act inhibited, while inexpressive students were always rated as more inhibited than expressive students, even when trying to act expressive. The students assigning the ratings weren't fooled by the students trying to act against their natural personality; the raters always saw expressive students as more animated than inexpressive students. The researchers concluded that it is very difficult for people to alter their behavior from their natural tendencies.[11] And even if we do manage to alter our behavior, we will never reach the level of someone to whom that behavior comes naturally. In other words, it's hard to be someone you're not!

Six Personality Traits

Once early psychologists discovered that people behave fairly consistently, they realized that everyone must be able to see these personality traits in themselves and others. And since we use words to describe what we see, all the common traits of people's personality must be reflected in human language. Hence, the search for personality traits began by reviewing the English dictionary and picking out all the different words used to describe people—friendly, argumentative, organized, emotional, and so on.[12]

As you can imagine, the English language has hundreds of words that describe people. Such a long list of personality traits would be difficult to manage, and even more difficult to apply in a useful way, so researchers looked for ways to narrow down the list to a set of fundamental attributes. By employing a statistical technique called factor analysis, they discovered that many of these words share meaning and are statistically related. Factor analysis revealed six underlying traits: *Curious*, *Organized*, *Caring*, *Outgoing*, *Ambitious*, and *Resilient*.[13] The core traits are easy to remember—just think "cocoa plus R." Every person has a combination of these six traits, and together they determine your natural behavioral tendencies, including what you enjoy doing and find intrinsically rewarding. Before you read any further, it's important that you understand where you fall on the spectrum of each of these six traits. You can go through the exercise included here in Figure 3-1, or you can take the longer Leader Habit Quiz for free at www.leaderhabit.com. (If you take the free Leader Habit Quiz online, you will also receive a ranking of the top twenty-two leadership skills

Figure 3-1 What's Your Personality?

Here are a series of phrases that describe people's behaviors. Please indicate how accurately each statement describes you by circling a number. Describe yourself as you generally are now, not as you wish to be in the future. Describe yourself as you honestly see yourself–there are no right or wrong answers. Please read each statement carefully and then circle the appropriate option on the scale.

I SEE MYSELF AS:	Very Inaccurate	Moderately Inaccurate	Neither Inaccurate nor Accurate	Moderately Accurate	Very Accurate
Open-minded, curious, and creative	1	2	3	4	5
Dependable, organized, and punctual	1	2	3	4	5
Warm, caring, and sympathetic	1	2	3	4	5
Friendly, outgoing, and not shy	1	2	3	4	5
Driven, ambitious, and decisive	1	2	3	4	5
Calm, resilient, and not easily stressed	1	2	3	4	5

The middle word in each phrase identifies the personality trait it measures. For example, "open-minded, curious, and creative" measures the trait Curious. If you circled 1 or 2, you are low on that trait, but if you circled 4 or 5, you are high on the trait. Response of 3 means that you are flexible and can easily fluctuate between high and low behaviors.

based on how they align with your personality. This ranking will help you select which skills to start with when you build your Leader Habit workout plan in Chapter 5.)

As you look at your personality results, note that you scored high on some traits and low on others. This is normal and expected. Your unique combination of traits is neither good nor bad—it's just who you are. Psychologists think of each trait as a continuum ranging from low to high. The closer you are to the middle of the continuum, the more flexible you generally are on that trait. As with anything in life, it's the extremes that raise red flags—when a person is too low or too high on the continuum for a particular trait, it may result in negative behaviors.

The main purpose of finding your personality traits is to help you determine which leadership skills come to you naturally and are intrinsically rewarding. Remember that intrinsic rewards are more effective at forming habits than extrinsic rewards, because intrinsic rewards don't lose their value—it's always satisfying to do what comes naturally to us. Furthermore, skills that align with your personality traits aren't just intrinsically rewarding, they also require less effort to practice, which, as you will see, is one of the keys to making your practice sustainable. The point is to use the insight into your personality traits to pick the leadership skills that you will enjoy working on, so that you can more easily turn them into habits.

In the following pages, I describe the six personality traits and highlight which leadership skills these traits influence. You will find more detail about the relationship between the six personality traits and the twenty-two leadership skills in Part III.

Curious

Curious leaders are strong strategists and visionaries who promote innovation and change. They enjoy solving complex problems and strategizing different business scenarios. Leaders who score high on Curious tend to be creative, intellectual types. They spend time contemplating ideas and often notice things that others don't. It is therefore no surprise that, out of all the traits, Curious had the strongest relationship with problem-solving skills in research.[14] Leadership skills like Analyze Information and Think Through Solutions come naturally to high scorers.

Individuals scoring high on Curious have a natural propensity to be good at innovation and strategic thinking. In research, Curious showed strong relationships with behaviors like offering ideas about new and different ways of doing things, discussing new ideas, encouraging thinking along new lines, experimenting with new ways of doing things, and seeing possibilities rather than problems.[15] Hence, leadership skills like Innovate come naturally to high scorers.

Leaders who score too high on Curious come off as abstract, idealistic, and too conceptual. They may spend most of their time contemplating and playing with their ideas, to the point that they cannot reach a decision. They may also struggle to make their ideas practical.

Leaders who are low on Curious are more practical, concrete, linear thinkers. Although they may be seen as less strategic, they tend to be sensible and pragmatic in their decision-making. Hence, leadership skills like Make Good Decisions and Manage Priorities come naturally to low scorers because they don't spend much time pondering tangential information and getting lost in their thoughts. Leaders who are too low on Curious tend to resist innovation and are reluctant to change or take risks.

Organized

Organized leaders plan well, follow rules, and deliver on time. They enjoy creating structures and processes and are naturally driven to create predictability in life. Compared to other traits, Organized has the strongest relationship with leadership skills that center around planning and organizing work for self and others.[16] High scorers are methodical, systematic, diligent, and reliable. They have plans and procedures for most aspects of their life and do their best to account for unforeseen setbacks ahead of time; their plans often go off without a hitch. Leadership skills like Plan and Organize Work and Manage Priorities come naturally to leaders scoring high on Organized.

In addition to leadership skills like setting clear goals and planning carefully, Organized also shows a strong relationship with analytical skills like analyzing information and thinking things through before deciding.[17] Organized leaders tend to be more linear in their thinking and they tend to follow a more systematic path in decision-making. As a result, leadership skills like Think Through Solutions and Make Good Decisions come more naturally to high scorers.

Leaders that are too high on Organized may be rigid, controlling, perfectionistic, and risk-averse. They can miss out on new opportunities that diverge from their plans because they are inflexible. Sometimes they adhere strictly to a schedule or a process and react negatively when minor issues arise or things do not go as planned. If you experience distress when obstacles create setbacks to your plans, you may be too high on Organized.

Leaders low on Organized are flexible and more tolerant of ambiguity. Leadership skills like Innovate and Delegate Well come more naturally to low scorers, as these skills require more openness, tolerance of ambiguity, flexibility, and abstract thinking. Leaders who are too low on Organized may become disorganized, unpredictable, less detail-oriented, and scattered.

Caring

Caring leaders value cooperation and getting along with their teams. They intuitively understand others' needs and readily provide support. Leaders who score high on Caring are perceptive, supportive, empathetic, and cooperative. Compared to all other traits, Caring showed the strongest relationship with behaviors related to consideration of others in research. Similarly, in another research study, Caring was strongly related to behaviors like being considerate and showing regard for employees as people, showing appreciation for their work, standing up for employees, and listening to their ideas and suggestions.[18] Leadership skills like Show Caring and Listen Actively come naturally to high scorers.

The leadership behaviors associated with leading teams tend to come naturally to individuals who score high on Caring. In a study of 126 managers and executives, Caring exhibited the strongest relationship with empowering others, supporting people, and participating in teamwork and activities.[19] Because of their considerate, supportive nature, high scorers tend to be naturally good at leadership skills like Build Team Spirit, Empower Others, and Mentor and Coach.

Leaders who score too high on Caring run the risk of being "too nice" and too eager to please others. Their desire to be liked may negatively affect their performance to the point that they are easily swayed and let others take advantage of them. They may actively avoid conflict and confrontations.

Leaders low on Caring are described as tolerant and accommodating. If they are too low on Caring, they become less cooperative, overly direct, and tough. Sometimes they may be seen as insensitive to others' feelings.

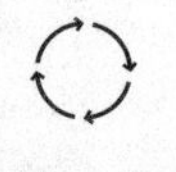

Outgoing

Outgoing leaders are charismatic, build rapport quickly, and communicate well. They enjoy teamwork and networking. Leaders who score high on Outgoing are charming, talkative, dynamic, and enthusiastic. As a result, they tend to have a natural advantage in communication and influencing skills. People generally like listening to such dynamic individuals and are more likely to retain what they say. Leadership skills like Speak with Charisma, Communicate Clearly, and Sell the Vision come naturally to high scorers because of their natural drive to express excitement and compel others to action.

Relationship-building behaviors come naturally to Outgoing leaders. Their charming style makes them good conversationalists, and they are able to quickly build rapport with others. In research, Outgoing showed the strongest relationship with having an open and honest style and being friendly, which further contributes to high scorers' ability to build strong relationships with people.[20] The leadership skill Build Strategic Relationships is a natural fit for high scorers.

People who are too high on Outgoing tend to be overly talkative and don't listen to others. In extreme cases, they may come off as brash, self-centered attention-seekers.

Leaders who score low on Outgoing are generally composed, reserved, and good listeners. They tend to observe and listen because of their reserved nature. Hence, leadership skills like Listen Actively and Negotiate Well come to them naturally.

Individuals who score too low on Outgoing are often seen as distant, withdrawn, and soft-spoken. These people may be impersonal and awkward in social settings, and it can be difficult to engage them in conversation.

Ambitious

Ambitious leaders make determined decisions and set stretch goals that they generally achieve. They are competitive and motivated by status. Leaders high on Ambitious are driven to achieve goals and are often the boldest person in the room. They take initiative and are confident, decisive, energetic, persuasive, and influential. This gives them a natural ability to influence others and lead change. In research, Ambitious showed strong relationships with pushing for growth, giving thoughts and plans about the future, and initiating new projects.[21] Leadership skills like Sell the Vision and Create Urgency come naturally to high scorers.

High scorers also tend to have the drive and confidence to make decisions even if they lack all the necessary information, and they are not struck by decision paralysis as often as lower scorers. Researchers have found that Ambitious is strongly related to taking risks in decisions and making quick decisions when necessary.[22] Leadership skills like Make Good Decisions come naturally to high scorers.

When leaders are too high on Ambitious, they may be seen as aggressive and overbearing. In extreme cases, this elevated ambition may lead them to make reckless decisions that are too risky for their business.

Leaders who score low on Ambitious are laid-back, unhurried, and reluctant to take charge. They often struggle to create a sense of urgency. If they're too low, they are seen as passive, hesitant, and indecisive. These leaders may often struggle with decision paralysis, feeling like they need to collect more information before they can make a decision.

Resilient

Resilient leaders persist to overcome obstacles, and they remain positive and confident when facing challenges. They are predictable and manage their emotions well. Leaders who score high on Resilient are calm, even-tempered, and cool under pressure. In research, Resilient was more strongly related than any other trait to tolerance of stress, pressure, opposition, disappointment, and uncertainty.[23] Their calm demeanor gives high scorers a natural advantage in difficult situations, so leadership skills like Overcome Individual Resistance will come naturally to them. Similarly, in negotiation situations, high scorers are able to keep their cool and thoughtfully find win-win opportunities under pressure, making them naturally good at leadership skills like Negotiate Well.

When leaders are too high on Resilient, their demeanor is often challenging for others to read, and as a result they can be seen as unemotional and difficult to connect with. In some cases, these leaders are overly confident to the point that they dismiss negative feedback and overlook the needs of others.

Leaders who score low on Resilient tend to be sensitive with frequently shifting emotional states. They are impatient, moody, and easily frustrated. Leaders who are too low on Resilient have a tendency to overreact to setbacks, become easily stressed, nervous, and worried. They may be perceived as volatile, negative, unpredictable, and lacking self-confidence.

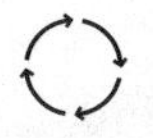

When It Comes to Practice, Less Is Always More

Now that you have some insight into your personality traits, you should be better prepared to identify which leadership skills you will find intrinsically rewarding. This will be important when it comes time to build your Leader Habit workout plan, because the skills that align with your personality will be easier to practice.

As I mentioned earlier, your ability to sustain the deliberate practice of a skill long enough to turn that skill into a habit is dependent on two things: how rewarding you find the skill *and* how much effort it takes for you to practice it. A common mistake is to assume that a high degree of intrinsic reward is all you need. This assumption overlooks the fact that even the most intrinsically rewarding activity requires *motivation* for us to follow through on it. If you don't have enough motivation to do something, you won't do it, no matter how much you enjoy it.

I experienced this with downhill skiing in my early twenties. I love skiing. It is so intrinsically rewarding to me that, during the winter months, I wake up before dawn on the weekends to head up to the mountains. But back in my college days, getting up early Saturday morning to go skiing was sometimes tough, especially after having a few drinks (or more than a few) with friends the night before. No matter how much I enjoyed skiing, the occasional Saturday hangover would keep me in bed late into the morning, and there were a few Saturdays when I never even made it to the slopes. Despite my love for the sport, my motivation was just too low on those days.

Motivation isn't constant, as you have no doubt experienced, and it is often difficult to predict when we will feel motivated and when we won't. But why? Is motivation determined by the activity we are doing? Do we lose motivation over time? Are some people constantly more motivated than others? Researchers at the University of Barcelona set out to answer these questions by studying how much people's motivation varied throughout the day and day over day.

In their study, the researchers asked employed adults to carry Personal Digital Assistants to complete a quick survey six times per day for twenty-one days. This method allowed for more accurate assessment of motivation in the moment, as opposed to asking the participants to reflect on the day after the fact. The sample was diverse, with participants holding a range of occupations including postmen, sports team managers, HR directors, bank employees, accountants, and farmers. Participants answered the same four questions on each survey: What activity are you doing right now? How much does it motivate you? How capable are you to do this activity? Is this activity bringing you closer to your personal goal?

The results of the study showed that people's motivation fluctuates quite a bit every day and from day to day *regardless of the type of activity they are doing.*[24] So it doesn't matter how intrinsically rewarding the activity is—during some moments of the day, your motivation is high and other times it's low. Similarly, on some days motivation is high, and on other days it is low, no matter how much you enjoy an activity or consciously want to do it. Perhaps you feel tired, or hungry, or bored, and these states influence the daily fluctuation in your motivation.

What does this mean when it comes to sustaining practice and developing leadership habits? Simply that you must plan for the days when your motivation is at its lowest level, so that you can complete your practice even when you don't have the energy to do anything else.

It turns out the best way to sustain your practice (especially on those days when you feel tired and unmotivated) is to *minimize* effort. Researchers at Maastricht University in the Netherlands discovered this by studying how students interacted with a basic computer game, called the Hurricane Game. In the Hurricane Game, players "catch" a fast-moving square that travels across the screen and appears every quarter of a second in a different place. Players stare at the screen waiting for the square to appear, and once the square is visible, they must click on it before it disappears again. The game requires a great deal of attention, focus, and hand-eye coordination. It has six levels of difficulty. As the level of difficulty increases, the square gets smaller and harder to spot. It's not the most exciting computer game, so the researchers paid the students $0.25 every time they successfully clicked on the square. Unknown to the students, the researchers were interested in the relationship between the difficulty level of the game and the motivation required to complete that level. In other words, do more difficult tasks require higher levels of motivation to perform than easier tasks?

As you might suspect, the answer is "yes." Only 29 percent of students attempted the game's most difficult level, while 99 percent attempted the easiest level.[25] When the game was too difficult, significantly fewer students attempted it—they lacked the motivation to try. Indeed, the more difficult a task is, the more motivation it requires. And when the task is too difficult, people just give up and they don't even make an attempt, just as the majority of the students didn't attempt the Hurricane Game's most difficult level.

This is why the Leader Habit Formula uses simple exercises to build habits. By making the exercises as easy as possible and only practicing a single exercise at a time, once per day, the effort required to sustain your practice is low, which means you should be able to complete your exercise even on those days when your motivation is at its all-time low. The Leader Habit Formula increases your chances of practice on days when you feel tired, stressed, hungry, or generally demotivated.

Just Five Minutes a Day

Remember Tristan Pang? He is the child prodigy from the beginning of this chapter who couldn't stop studying mathematics and physics. He thoroughly enjoyed the subjects and quickly developed expertise in them to the point that he by far surpassed most of his peers. While his peers are still in high school, Tristan is already attending Auckland

College. Outside of his love for mathematics, there is something else that distinguishes Tristan from his peers—when it comes to math and physics, he doesn't procrastinate.

As you may know from personal experience, procrastination is a serious issue in academia; it affects between 70–95 percent of undergraduate students.[26] "I'll do it tomorrow" is a common attitude most of us experienced at one point or another when it came to homework. But procrastination leads to many negative outcomes, such as cramming the night before finals, submitting late homework, test anxiety, and low GPA. So why do we procrastinate?

At the University of Alberta, researchers wanted to understand why undergraduate students procrastinate and what factors lead them to deliberately avoid homework and assignments. By surveying 261 students, they found that the strongest individual predictor of procrastination was students' belief in their own capability to do their schoolwork: Students who didn't believe that they were capable of the schoolwork procrastinated more than those who believed they could do the work.[27] It's the belief that you cannot do something that leads you to procrastinate. Indeed, it's difficult to feel motivated or excited to do something that you don't think you are good at.

Everyone procrastinates to some degree. Outside of education, procrastination seems to be especially prevalent in housecleaning, at least in my experience. How many times have you actively avoided dusting, loading the dishwasher, doing laundry, or vacuuming? If you are like me, housecleaning chores are where procrastination rules. It's not that we believe that we are incapable of doing the work—we certainly have the ability to clean the house. Instead our procrastination is fueled by another, related belief—that completing the task will take too much time. Overwhelmed by the thought of spending an entire Saturday doing chores, we think, "I'll do it tomorrow." Then when tomorrow comes, we think up a long list of activities to do instead. Day by day, the dust and clutter in our houses accumulates and the task of cleaning it up gets bigger and requires more and more time, encouraging us to procrastinate even more.

At some point, you have to break the cycle and start cleaning or risk becoming a hoarder. But how do you do it, when the task only seems to get more difficult the longer you procrastinate? Based on what we know about procrastination, the change has to occur in your thinking—you have to start believing that housecleaning is manageable and won't take too much time. You have to make the task seem smaller by tricking your brain into seeing it differently.

In their book *Switch*, Chip and Dan Heath introduced the world to Marla Cilley, a home-organizing coach, and her "5-Minute Room Rescue" system. Marla devised a brilliant strategy to break the house-cleaning-procrastination cycle. Here's how it works: You pick a room of your house, set a timer for five minutes, and get to work. When the timer goes off, you stop. Simple enough, right? No matter how dirty your house is, you can find the motivation to clean up for five minutes. And sure enough, people who tried this method stopped procrastinating and actually spent five minutes cleaning. Better yet, when they noticed how much they were able to achieve in those five minutes, they continued to clean longer. Pretty soon, their houses were spick-and-span.[28]

In the Hurricane Game experiment, when people thought the task was too difficult, the majority gave up and didn't even attempt it. In the case of undergraduate students, those who didn't believe that they were good at schoolwork procrastinated. In both examples, motivation was determined by people's thoughts—what they believed about the task in front of them. This insight applies to sustaining practice and building Leader Habits, too. In order to avoid the procrastination cycle, you must believe (*without* tricking your brain) that you can do your exercise every day, no matter what.

When writing the exercises for the Leader Habit Formula, my team and I were inspired by Marla's 5-Minute Room Rescue concept, and we deliberately set out to create exercises that would take five minutes or less to complete, so that busy, working adults would believe (correctly) they could actually do them.

Easy Does It

Developing leadership skills and turning them into habits takes time and sustained practice, but that doesn't mean the process has to be difficult. In fact, the opposite is true: The secret to sustaining your practice is to make it as easy as possible—and that's exactly what the Leader Habit Formula does.

The easiest way to sustain practice is to practice things that are intrinsically rewarding to you—think of Tristan Pang studying hour after hour to master thirteen years of mathematics curricula by age eleven. The concepts were often difficult at first, but learning them was so deeply satisfying to Tristan that he entered a flow state where the act of studying for hours on end felt effortless and enjoyable. To understand which leadership skills are intrinsically rewarding for you, look to your personality traits. Behaviors that align with our personality are satisfying; it feels good to do what comes naturally to us, and leadership skills are no exception.

Motivation is also an important factor in sustaining practice, because even highly rewarding activities require us to be motivated to do them. Remember that your motivation varies from day to day and hour to hour, regardless of what you're doing. And remember that the motivation required to complete a task is proportional to the difficulty of the task, meaning more difficult tasks require more motivation, and if a task is too difficult, you won't even attempt it. To keep the motivation threshold as low as possible, the Leader Habit exercises are simple and focus on only one small behavior at a time.

The Leader Habit exercises aren't just simple, they're also short. No matter how busy you are, you can spare five minutes a day to practice a simple exercise. If you can practice a simple exercise every day, you can develop a new leadership skill. And if you practice that skill every day for enough days in a row, that skill will become a habit. It's that easy.

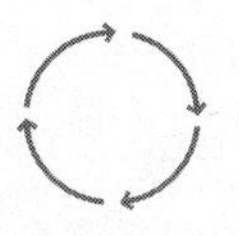

CHAPTER 4

From 5-Minute Exercise to Full-Blown Skill

When my neighbor Sabrina rescued a one-year-old golden retriever named Max from the dog pound, she had no idea what she was getting into. Max was Sabrina's first dog since she had moved out of her parent's house, so of course she spoiled the pup with all the toys you can imagine. Max's precious possessions included a rubber bone, squeaking chicken, cotton rope, plush beaver, rabbit, tennis ball, and more. Max thoroughly enjoyed all his toys, but Sabrina quickly discovered a problem: Max was a messy roommate. While Sabrina was at work, Max would play with his toys and scatter them all over the house, and being a dog, he never cleaned up after himself.

Fed up with always having to pick up Max's toys, Sabrina decided she would teach the dog to clean up his own mess. Sabrina knew Max was smart, and she knew dogs could be trained to do a lot of surprising things, so it didn't seem unreasonable to expect that Max could learn to put away his toys.

The first time Sabrina asked Max to "clean up," she received a confused stare. Max had never heard this command before, so he sat down. The next time he heard "clean up," Max tried barking—again, not the response Sabrina wanted. Max was eager to do his job, but he had no idea what that job was.

Sabrina didn't give up. She understood that cleaning up toys scattered around the house is a complex skill involving many steps. To "clean up,"

Max would have to locate a specific object (one of his toys, as opposed to one of Sabrina's shoes), walk to it, pick it up, carry it to the bin, and drop it in the bin. Then Max would have to start all over again with another toy, and he would have to repeat the process until all of the toys were in the bin. Sabrina understood this wasn't something Max could learn by simply hearing "clean up" over and over again; it was going to take a more deliberate approach. She did some research into how to train complex skills and found a YouTube video by dog trainer Pamela Johnson.[1] Then she went to work training Max to clean up his toys.

Max's "clean-up" training regime consisted of five exercises, which Sabrina practiced with him one at a time in sequence. The first exercise taught Max a simple behavior—*take and drop*. Sabrina handed Max a toy, Max took it in his mouth, and then Sabrina waited until Max dropped the toy on the floor or in her hand. With every correct response, Max received a treat. After several repetitions, Max got the hang of it, and soon he was taking and dropping the toys consistently when asked. That's when Sabrina introduced the second exercise—*take and drop into the bin*.

For the second exercise, Max would practice taking and dropping his toys into the plastic bin where he was supposed to keep all his toys. Sabrina set the empty bin in one corner of the room and led Max over to it. Then she handed Max a toy and asked him to drop it. Since the bin was right there, it was easy for Max to drop his toy into the bin. To make sure that Max understood that he was meant to drop his toy into the bin, Sabrina also placed the treat into the bin. Max quickly realized that there would be a treat for him in the bin, if he dropped his toy there. It wasn't long before Max was consistently dropping his toys into the bin and it was time to move on to the third exercise.

The third exercise introduced a new twist—now Max had to take the toy and carry it across the room to the bin. With the bin still placed in the same corner, Sabrina stood in the opposite corner of the room and handed a toy to Max. Sabrina then walked over to the bin and Max followed her. When Sabrina asked him to drop the toy, Max anticipated that the treat would be in the bin. And so Max learned to carry a toy across the room and drop it into the bin.

In the fourth exercise, Sabrina placed different toys around the room and Max's task was to pick up each toy, carry it across the room, and drop it into the bin. Sabrina would stand next to a toy and ask Max to pick it up and take it to the bin. By now Max knew a treat awaited him in the bin, so he eagerly picked up each toy and carried it across the room, as he had learned to do in the previous exercise. Max quickly understood that he was meant to pick up all the different toys and carry them to the bin.

Finally, for the fifth exercise, Sabrina introduced the command "clean up" as the cue for Max's new behavior. In almost no time, Max would respond to the cue by running to the first toy he saw, picking it up, and carrying it to the bin. Once the cue was set, the training was complete. And now Max cleans up his toys on command.

Leadership Skills Are Chains of Micro-Behaviors

Through a series of simple exercises, Sabrina had successfully taught Max a complex behavior that would have been difficult, if not impossible, for the dog to learn otherwise. The technique Sabrina used is called *chaining*, and by now you should recognize it as a key part of the Leader Habit Formula. This popular and effective technique is used in Applied Behavior Analysis to teach animals, children, and adults complex skills. The principles of chaining are simple and intuitive: first, break down the complex behavior into its constituent micro-behaviors; then practice each micro-behavior separately; and finally combine the micro-behaviors together to form the complex skill.[2]

Many of the complex skills you hold today you acquired through chaining, whether you realize it or not. If you ever played piano, think back to how you learned a new composition. First, you split the piece into smaller sections. Then you practiced the right-hand and left-hand parts for the first section separately. Once you could play those parts separately, you put them together and practiced until you could play the first section with both hands. Then you repeated the process with each section until you could play the whole piece.

Or think back to learning a sport, like tennis. You didn't learn all the strokes at once, because that would have been too difficult. So you practiced your forehand first, then your backhand, then you learned to serve, and finally you worked on putting all the strokes together in a game.

Even assembling IKEA furniture or LEGO toys is a form of chaining: You follow step-by-step instructions that break down a complex assembly process into a sequence of simple micro-behaviors.

Why is chaining such an effective technique? Because, as we learned from the transatlantic submarine voyage simulation in Chapter 2, simple behaviors turn into habits faster than complex behaviors. It's much easier to learn each micro-behavior separately and then chain them together than it is to try to learn the entire complex sequence of micro-behaviors at once. Most people intuitively understand this, and most of us have used chaining to successfully learn many complex skills; and yet the standard approach in leadership development programs is to expect trainees to immediately acquire complex leadership skills all at once.

In my research described in Chapter 2, my team and I identified the micro-behaviors that make up the twenty-two most common leadership skills. For example, we found that leaders who Delegate Well practice the following behaviors: (1) they delegate a project that fits the person's skills; (2) they consider the person's interests when delegating a task or project; and (3) they identify what is to be accomplished and let the person figure out how to accomplish it. In order to develop the skill of delegating well, you must master all of these behaviors and turn them into habits. Of course, you could try to practice them all at once, but that goes against everything we have learned about the ways that people most effectively acquire new skills and form new habits. It would be like

Sabrina trying to teach Max all the steps of "clean up" at the same time, or trying to learn a Beethoven piano sonata all the way through from start to finish.

The Leader Habit Formula takes advantage of the power of chaining. Each micro-behavior that makes up a leadership skill has its own targeted 5-minute exercise, and you practice each micro-behavior separately, using the appropriate exercise, until it turns into a habit. Then you move on to daily practice of the next micro-behavior and so on until all the targeted behaviors have become habits. In this way you build a complex skill, like delegating well, as a chain of micro-behaviors. The short, simple exercises enable you to focus on one piece of the puzzle at a time, rather than trying to tackle the much more difficult task of learning all the components of the complex skill simultaneously.

While chaining is simple and effective, it does have one drawback: It is a linear process that assumes each micro-behavior must be practiced and mastered one at a time, and all the micro-behaviors of a particular skill must be mastered before you can move on to the next skill. This limitation wouldn't be a concern if there were only a few skills and micro-behaviors involved in becoming a better leader, but remember there are twenty-two leadership skills made up of seventy-nine micro-behaviors, and we need to spend an average of sixty-six days practicing each micro-behavior. That works out to *over fourteen years of practice* to turn every leadership micro-behavior into a habit. Who has that much time? Even if you were the most dedicated and motivated person in the world, you probably wouldn't make it through all twenty-two skills. What we need is a shortcut, something that accelerates your leadership development.

Fortunately there is such a shortcut, as Charles Duhigg discusses in his best-selling book *The Power of Habit*. This shortcut happens when a single habit triggers a chain reaction of behavioral change that transforms many different aspects of your life. Duhigg calls it a *keystone habit*.[3]

The Making of a Keystone Habit

When I first met John, he was convinced that he had all the necessary skills to step into an executive role right then and there. He had been successful in management positions for several years, and he knew the ins and outs of his organization as well as anyone. A promotion to the C-suite was a given in his mind. But in reality the situation wasn't quite that simple. John, like Laura the ER nurse, had a bad habit that was holding him back, and he didn't realize it. He would need to make a drastic change if he wanted to be an executive. That's when I started working with him.

John was described to me by his colleagues and the employees he managed as domineering and authoritarian, and I quickly realized why: When people raised concerns to him about projects, initiatives, and assignments, John always downplayed or dismissed those concerns. Whether it was in one-on-one conversations, in meetings, or at home, John didn't seem to care when people weren't on board with his plans. He expected everyone to trust his judgment and do as he said because he was in charge.

As a result, John's colleagues, friends, and family members had begun to resent him when he gave orders. Most of the time they would comply with his requests, but they weren't fully engaged because they didn't feel they had a personal stake in what he was asking them to do.

John's authoritarian behavior was undermining many critical leadership skills. He couldn't effectively influence other people, overcome resistance, negotiate, or coach and mentor them. If he didn't drop this bad habit, he would never become an effective leader.

When I explained the concept of leadership development as a simple 5-minute daily exercise, John was skeptical, as Laura the ER nurse had been, but he agreed to give it a try. After some deliberation, he settled on an exercise to help him make a habit of asking people about their concerns: *After someone expresses a concern or dissatisfaction, ask a targeted question to better understand the person's position by saying, "What makes you concerned about this?"*

At first the exercise was uncomfortable for John. His habit of ignoring or dismissing others' concerns was deeply ingrained, so he had to consciously stop himself from doing it. But he found that he was able to sustain his practice because the exercise itself was so simple (ask a question), he only had to remember to do it once a day, and it didn't take long to complete. And sure enough, after about two months, John and the people around him began to notice a change in his behavior—he was acknowledging people's concerns and taking them seriously. The more he practiced his simple exercise, the more John noticed how much more engaged other people were when they felt their concerns were being heard. He started encountering less resistance to his plans and ideas; his employees were more engaged with their work and showed him more respect; and he found that he had more influence among his fellow managers. Soon he was proactively asking people to share their concerns, rather than waiting for them to speak up. His new habit was formed.

The changes that resulted from John's new habit didn't stop there. The simple act of asking other people about their concerns caused other leadership skills to blossom—skills he hadn't yet deliberately practiced. Within a year, John was promoted to an executive position. Soon after his promotion, John had to give negative feedback to a new director in his group who was not performing well. He was anxious about the situation because in the past he hadn't handled giving negative feedback well. But John quickly discovered that it didn't matter. When he sat down with the underperforming director, his new habit automatically took over: Instead of taking a stern, authoritarian approach, he simply stated the facts and then asked the director what concerns he had about his own performance.

Before he knew it, John was engaging the director in an effective coaching discussion. The director shared his experiences in his new job, his understanding of his shortcomings, and where he thought he could improve—and best of all, he came up with good ideas about how to do his job more effectively. John's new habit had spread beyond the skill of influencing others—he was now also getting better at mentoring and coaching, even though he hadn't explicitly practiced this skill.

For John, the behavior he learned from the "ask about concerns" exercise became his keystone habit. Once it took root, it spread and changed other behaviors that improved other leadership skills. John quickly became better at influencing people, overcoming resistance, negotiating, and coaching his employees. These same skills also transformed his friendships and family relationships. All because a single 5-minute exercise created a keystone habit.

From 5-Minute Exercise to Complete Transformation

The Leader Habit Formula can help you learn any new leadership habit. However, the Formula is most effective if you use it to build a keystone habit first. If you can build a keystone habit, it will accelerate your leadership development process. In order to identify which habits might be good candidates for your own keystone habit, it helps to understand how keystone habits trigger such dramatic and far-reaching changes.

Psychologists have discovered the principles that explain how keystone habits work. To begin with, remember the chronic procrastination of the undergraduates who kept putting off homework and the reluctance of the experiment participants who didn't have the motivation to attempt the Hurricane Game's most difficult level. The reason the procrastinating students actively avoided homework and the players didn't attempt the most difficult level was that they didn't believe in their own ability; they didn't think that they would be good at the task they had been asked to complete. In psychological terms, their *self-efficacy* was low. When people's self-efficacy is low, their motivation is also low and they generally avoid the activity they think they aren't good enough to succeed at, either by procrastinating or giving up entirely.[4] In order to increase their motivation, people have to start believing that they can actually do the activity—their self-efficacy has to increase.

Marla Cilley's 5-Minute Room Rescue technique got people to stop procrastinating and clean their houses because it does just that. By shrinking chores to just five minutes per day, people come to believe that they can do it—after all, it's just five minutes. More importantly, after they spend five minutes cleaning, people realize how much they are able to accomplish in that short time, and their confidence in their ability increases.[5]

Similarly, after just a few repetitions of his Leader Habit exercise, John realized that he truly was capable of doing it—he could ask people about their concerns and learn to hear and acknowledge those concerns. The 5-minute exercise brought him a "small win" every single day, which motivated him to keep practicing. Soon the exercise wasn't just about asking people to share their concerns; it became an exercise in building his self-efficacy. Every time he practiced, John became more confident in his ability to get better at influencing other people, which made it easier for him to change other behaviors as well.

The simple "ask about concerns" exercise became John's keystone habit because he was practicing both the overt behavior—hearing and acknowledging concerns—and also using his willpower. Every day, with every repetition of his new behavior, his willpower grew stronger. Realizing that he could actually do this increased his self-efficacy, which in turn gave him the confidence to continue developing other leadership skills. The simple, 5-minute exercise had started an avalanche of change.

But this type of change doesn't happen on its own—there are several conditions necessary for a habit to become a keystone habit.

It Matters Where You Practice

In 1975, researchers at the University of Stirling ran one of the more famous experiments in psychology. Near the port town of Oban in

Scotland, they played recordings of a list of words to scuba divers while the divers were submerged ten feet underwater. The divers had been asked beforehand to try to memorize the words they heard. When the divers surfaced and returned to the beach, the researchers tested their ability to recall the words and recorded how many words each diver remembered.

For a second group of divers, the researchers prepared a slightly different test. After listening to the initial list of words underwater, these divers were asked to swim a short distance, dive twenty feet, and then return to the original position before attempting to recall the words. The important difference between the two scenarios is that the second group was tested underwater rather than on the beach; they were asked to recall the words in the same environment where they learned them.

The results were surprising—divers recalled more words underwater than on land.[6] Their ability to recall what they had learned was influenced by where they were asked to remember it. The divers remembered more words when they were located in the same environment where the learning occurred. Once on land, they couldn't remember as much.

The explanation for this surprising effect can be traced back to automaticity, the same psychological principle that is responsible for habit formation. As you know, our brains automatically process information without our conscious awareness, and it turns out that some of this information gets unconsciously stored along with our memories. For instance, your brain is now automatically analyzing the space where you are sitting and reading this book. You don't need to pay attention to this process for it to happen; your brain is storing the information automatically, and you will remember tomorrow where you read this chapter.

As part of your memory of this chapter, your brain is effortlessly remembering the different cues about your environment. Is it dark or light, warm or cold, quiet or loud? Are you alone or are other people around you? What sounds are you hearing? What colors are you seeing?

All of this information is stored as part of your memory of this moment, and when you find yourself in a similar environment, all these cues will prompt your brain to surface the memory to your conscious awareness, making it easier to recall.

This explains why the divers in the experiment remembered more words underwater—it was the same environment where they had heard the words. When they were back on dry land, all the environmental cues their brains had unconsciously stored along with the memory of the words were gone, so it was more difficult for them to remember the words. This phenomenon came to be known as *context effect*, and it is the reason why it's so difficult to remember concepts you learn in the classroom outside of it. Context effects are also a nemesis of keystone habits because they can limit a habit to being triggered only in one particular situation, which is the opposite of what needs to happen.

For a habit to become your keystone habit, it must be able to spread into many domains of your life; that means it can't be limited to just one type of scenario or environment by context effects. For example, John's habit of asking about concerns wouldn't have been transformative if he had used it in staff meetings but not in one-on-one conversations, or if it had only changed his behavior in professional settings and not with his friends and family.

Context effects happen as part of natural processing of information, but there is an easy way to overcome them: practice your 5-minute daily exercise in many different environments. Make it a point to practice in your office and at home, in your hotel room and on the plane while traveling, on your laptop and your desktop, in meetings and around the dinner table, with colleagues and friends and family members . . . you get the idea. By changing where and with whom you practice your 5-minute exercise, you are fighting context effects and increasing the power of the behavior you are practicing to help you become a better leader all around—and you are increasing the chances of that behavior becoming your keystone habit.

One Good Habit Leads to Another

Before automobile manufacturers began installing seat belt warning chimes in most vehicles, pizza delivery drivers rarely buckled up. Because they were racing against time trying to satisfy hungry customers and constantly jumping in and out of their vehicles, wearing a seat belt wasn't the drivers' top priority. In fact, the business of fast pizza delivery gained a reputation for reckless driving. The combination of low seat belt use and higher-risk driving behaviors posed a serious health threat to the drivers and was a liability to the businesses.

Behavior analysts at Virginia Polytechnic Institute designed an intervention to increase the use of seat belts among pizza delivery drivers. After a brief discussion with the drivers about the benefits of wearing a seat belt, they installed buckle-up reminder signs in two pizza stores. The signs were meant to serve as cues in the habit-building process. After the intervention, the researchers secretly observed the drivers from strategic positions with a clear view of the parking lot located by the two pizza stores.

What the researchers observed was remarkable. Not only were the drivers buckling up more often after the intervention, but some even started using turn signals more frequently.[7] Although using turn signals was not part of the intervention, and no reminders were placed in the pizza stores to encourage drivers to use them, for some drivers the seat belt intervention led to other safe driving behaviors. How did this happen?

The answer can be found in the relationship between the two behaviors. If we were to divide all driving behaviors into two groups, one representing safe driving behaviors and the other unsafe behaviors, wearing a seat belt and using turn signals would both be in the safe group. Even though the specific actions of each behavior are different, conceptually they are related. Because the two behaviors are related, it was possible for the trained behavior (buckling up) to unconsciously influence the drivers to perform another related behavior (using turn signals). Notice, for example, that the drivers who began wearing a seat belt didn't all of a sudden also start eating healthier or going to the gym. Those health behaviors belong to a different conceptual group, so developing a new habit of seat belt use won't affect them one way or the other. These findings provide insight into another important aspect of keystone habits: they usually spread into conceptually related behaviors, and not outside of their domain.

A few decades before the pizza delivery seat belt intervention, psychologists at Stanford University discovered the psychological process that explains how one habit can influence another. The researchers, posing as volunteers, went door to door in a residential neighborhood asking homeowners to display an ugly, very large sign on their front lawn that read, "Drive Carefully." The request was deliberately ridiculous, as the sign was large enough to obscure the house behind it, and so it should come as no surprise that a large majority of homeowners refused to display the sign.

There was, however, one group of homeowners that agreed to the researchers' request and offered their front lawns for installation of the massive sign. These same homeowners had been visited two weeks earlier by a different researcher also posing as a volunteer. This researcher also asked this group of homeowners to display a safe-driving sign, but the request was very small—the sign was just three inches tall. Most homeowners in this group agreed to display the tiny sign. They had no idea how much this decision would influence their future behavior, and they certainly wouldn't have predicted that two weeks later they would agree to have a massive billboard installed on their front lawn.[8]

The reason why homeowners who agreed to display the small sign also agreed to the massive billboard is that their small initial commitment changed how they viewed themselves—it changed their self-image. By agreeing to display the small sign, they came to see themselves as advocates for safe driving. Once this became part of how they saw themselves, it was only natural for them to agree to other signs that were consistent with their new self-image.

Similarly, the pizza delivery drivers who started buckling up came to see themselves as safer drivers. As their self-image changed, their other driving behaviors changed to match it.

Never underestimate the power of a behavior, no matter how small it might seem. When you start practicing one of the 5-minute Leader Habit exercises, your new behavior can become a keystone habit that causes you to change a whole set of related behaviors. What started for John as a simple exercise in asking about others' concerns also improved his other leadership skills. By learning to hear and acknowledge concerns, he not only became better at influencing people, but he also improved at overcoming resistance to change, negotiating, and mentoring and coaching. He improved these skills because they are conceptually related to the skill he was practicing. He needed to be able to hear why someone was reluctant to make a change before he could overcome their resistance to it and convince the person to accept the new course of action. He needed to give his employees an opportunity to express their concerns and reservations before he could effectively coach them.

John's simple exercise also changed his self-image: By deliberately and consistently practicing the behavior, he started to see himself as a better "people leader." This made it possible for his new habit to start the chain reaction that spread to other leadership skills. Day by day, little by little, his keystone habit was helping him to change a whole range of related behaviors to match his new self-image, which accelerated his leadership development.

Two Groups of Leadership Skills

The shortcut to rapid leadership development is finding your keystone habit. The idea that one new habit can trigger so many changes may seem too good to be true, but remember that habits have the power to influence conceptually related behaviors. As we saw with the pizza delivery drivers, an intervention designed to get them to buckle up also resulted in some drivers spontaneously starting to use their turn signals more. The important thing to keep in mind when thinking about how keystone habits accelerate change is that other desirable behaviors have to be related to the keystone habit.

As part of my research study, my team and I tested the relationships between the twenty-two leadership skills to identify the micro-behaviors that have the highest chance of becoming keystone habits. Remember that we had observed and analyzed the behavior of almost eight hundred leaders from around the world and rated each leader on the many micro-behaviors that make up the twenty-two leadership skills. In our statistical analysis of these ratings, we found that some skills were more strongly correlated to others. A strong positive correlation between two skills meant that if a leader had one skill, she was also more likely to have the other skill—a necessary condition for either skill to become a keystone habit.

Next we used factor analysis to examine the relationships between the set of leadership skills as a whole to see if some skills were more closely related than others. We found that the leadership skills clustered into two distinct groups. We called the first group *getting things done* and the second group *focusing on people.*

The distinction we identified between task-oriented and people-oriented leadership behaviors is not new. In fact, it was reported as early as 1955 by researchers at Ohio State University, who observed that some leaders focus on achieving results, while other leaders are more concerned about their people. Task-oriented leaders tend to initiate structure for their team, plan and organize work, delegate, monitor progress of employees, and push to get the job done. People-oriented leaders tend to focus on supporting and developing their employees, showing consideration, and motivating them.[9]

Once you understand the difference between task-oriented leadership and people-oriented leadership, it's only natural to wonder which style is better. Can you get more done by focusing on the results? Or is it more effective to focus on the people? This is a dilemma most leaders will face at one point or another in their careers. Many people intuitively choose to be task-oriented because it seems obvious that you should stress tasks and results if you want to achieve deadlines and goals.

It turns out the answer is not that straightforward. In a review of 231 studies of leadership behaviors, researchers at the University of Central Florida found that, although both task-oriented and people-oriented leadership behaviors had a positive impact on team productivity, focusing on people actually resulted in slightly higher team productivity than focusing on results. The researchers also found that only people-oriented leadership behaviors resulted in team learning; when leaders focused only on achieving results, their teams didn't learn.[10] To achieve the best results, leaders need both groups of skills—effective leaders must get things done *while* focusing on people.

Your Keystone Habits

What does all of this mean for your keystone habits? First, keep in mind that a keystone habit is most likely to start a chain reaction of behavior changes within the group of leadership skills where it conceptually belongs. For example, if you develop a task-oriented skill like Manage Priorities, the habit will likely spread to related skills, such as Plan and Organize Work, Create Urgency, Analyze Information, Make Good Decisions, or Delegate Well, because all of these skills focus on getting things done. But the same habit is unlikely to influence people-oriented behaviors like Listen Actively, Show Caring, or Mentor and Coach.

Second, remember that great leaders have skills that belong to both groups—they get things done while focusing on people. Based on the situation, they automatically respond with their habitual behaviors, sometimes providing support and other times cracking the whip. In order to be a great leader, you, too, will need to develop skills in both *getting things done* and *focusing on people*, so you will likely need to establish at least two keystone habits, one that helps accelerate your development of skills in each group. I will talk more about how to identify which exercises are most likely to become your keystone habits in the next chapter, when I discuss in detail how to plan your Leader Habit workout.

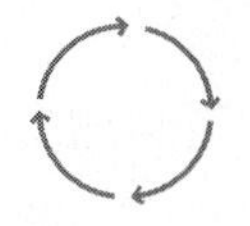

CHAPTER 5

Starting Your Leader Habit Workout

Now that you understand the Leader Habit Formula, it's time to build your Leader Habit workout.

Notice that I said *workout*. I chose that word to remind you that the Leader Habit Formula is about acquiring and strengthening skills through deliberate practice. It's no different than building physical strength by targeting specific muscle groups: If you want to become a better leader, you have to practice exercises that target specific leadership skills. Reading this book and learning about skills and micro-behaviors isn't enough. You have to put together a workout plan that will help you develop the skills you need to lead, and you have to do the workout long enough for your new skills to become habits.

But where to begin? There are twenty-two leadership skills and seventy-nine different exercises, each focused on a unique micro-behavior. With so many options to choose from, selecting your first exercise can feel overwhelming. Don't worry. The key to successful development is finding the overlap between the skills where you can grow and those that come naturally to you; that is where you will find the easiest and fastest growth—and your keystone habit. This chapter will help you identify those places of overlap, so that you can get your Leader Habit workout off to the strongest possible start.

Choose Your First Exercise Wisely

Your first Leader Habit exercise is the most important, because it has the power to make or break your entire leadership development workout. If you pick the right exercise, the behavior you practice will become a keystone habit that triggers a cascade of positive changes to related behaviors and increases your self-efficacy, making it easier to sustain your workout and helping you to build other skills faster. But if you pick the wrong exercise, the process will feel difficult instead of easy, you will struggle to practice on a daily basis, and eventually you will give up. Giving up is the opposite of successful leadership development, so let's look at some ways you can identify which exercises have the best potential to become your keystone habit.

In my line of work, we spend a considerable amount of time assessing clients to understand what leadership habits they already have, what comes naturally to them, and what micro-behaviors are most likely to become their keystone habits. We place clients in simulated business scenarios in a fictitious company, expose them to various cues, and observe how they respond. For instance, clients are asked to create a vision and strategy presentation for the fictitious company, and we have them role-play difficult scenarios, like coaching an underperforming employee or appeasing an angry customer. We observe how clients interact with live, human actors over a webcam and how they respond to urgent emails from their fictitious coworkers. All of this data allows us to precisely measure their current leadership skills and identify which skills need more practice.

In these simulations, we study the consistency of each leadership behavior in multiple different scenarios. We vary the cues and the response formats to measure if each micro-behavior suffers from context effects, like the scuba divers unable to remember on land what they had learned underwater. For example, a leader may be great at influencing others when she speaks to them in meetings, but she struggles to exert that same influence in email messages. In such cases, where a behavior is present but not yet consistent, the behavior in question is often a good candidate for the client's first Leader Habit exercise. Starting your workout by practicing something that you already do in one context is much easier than learning a totally new behavior.

When considering which Leader Habit exercise would be best for a client to start with, we also study how the client's personality aligns with each of the twenty-two leadership skills. If a person doesn't display a particular skill, we look at the relevant personality traits to understand how easy it will be for her to practice that skill. For example, if a client is not communicating clearly, we look at how she scored on the Organized trait to understand if the skill is something she can easily develop. If the client is low on Organized, it's unlikely that she would succeed in practicing an exercise that targets the micro-behavior of organizing a message around key points. This exercise wouldn't feel natural to the client and she wouldn't derive much intrinsic reward from it, which would make it difficult for her to keep practicing. Instead we would look for a skill that is aligned with the client's personality traits, which would be easier and more satisfying for her to do.

Simulation-based assessments are an effective way to identify potential keystone habits, but I know it's not always possible to prepare for your Leader Habit workout this way. If you don't have the opportunity to complete a simulation-based assessment, you can still be successful at choosing the right exercise to start your workout.

What You're Good at, What Comes Naturally, and Where You Can Grow

Without a simulation-based assessment to guide you, your biggest challenge will be correctly identifying which leadership skills you need to practice. This challenge arises because people are generally unaware of their true strengths and weaknesses. Remember how Laura and John didn't realize their bad habits? They both thought they were ready to take on more leadership responsibility, but their coworkers and superiors didn't see them as good leaders because of glaring weaknesses that Laura and John didn't recognize in themselves.

Researchers at the University of New South Wales and the University of Sydney studied just how much our own views of our strengths and weaknesses differ from how our colleagues see us. The researchers asked sixty-three team leaders at a large Australian service company to rate themselves on eleven leadership skills, such as planning and organizing, coaching people, making decisions, building relationships, and customer focus. Then they asked other people working with these team leaders to also rate them on the same leadership skills. These other people included the team leaders' bosses, peers, and the employees they supervised.

To their surprise, the researchers found no relationship between a person's self-assessment and how other people rated that person's leadership skills—the team leaders and their colleagues did not agree on the leaders' strengths and weaknesses.[1] The findings of this research might seem discouraging, especially when you are trying to build your Leader Habit workout plan. If it's difficult to accurately assess your own strengths and weaknesses, how do you know which skills you actually need to develop, and how can you hope to make a wise choice for your first exercise?

You're going to ask other people for input.

This is a two-step process. First, complete the questionnaire in Figure 5-1. The questions highlight the differences between the two broad categories of leadership skills, *getting things done* and *focusing on people*, which you can use as an initial filter to help you narrow down the choices for your first Leader Habit exercise. Your answers to these questions should give you a sense of whether you see yourself as being stronger on task-oriented or people-oriented leadership. This is your self-assessment baseline. It might be correct, or it might not—you can't be sure one way or the other because you are not the best judge of your own skills. (That's why this is a two-step process.)

Figure 5-1 What's Your Leadership Style?		
The questions below highlight the differences between the two broad categories of leadership skills, *getting things done* and *focusing on people*. Answers to these questions should give you a sense of whether you see yourself as being stronger on task-oriented or people-oriented leadership. Describe yourself as you generally are now, not as you wish to be in the future. Describe yourself as you honestly see yourself–there are no right and wrong answers.		
1. Do you see yourself more:		
❑ as a taskmaster	OR	❑ supporter of people around you?
2. Are you more likely to:		
❑ plan activities for others	OR	❑ encourage them to do what they want?
3. Do you find yourself worrying more about:		
❑ achieving results	OR	❑ maintaining harmony with your team?
4. Are you more likely to:		
❑ clarify who should do what	OR	❑ recognize people for what they have achieved so far?
5. Are you more likely to:		
❑ make the decisions for your team	OR	❑ empower them to take the initiative and decide for themselves?
If you have three or more selections in the left column, you see yourself as stronger on *getting things done*. But if you have three or more sections in the right column, you see yourself as stronger on *focusing on people*. This is your self-assessment baseline. It might be correct, or it might not–you can't be sure one way or the other because you are not the best judge of your own skills. That's why you should also ask at least two people that know you well and whose judgment you trust to answer the same questions about you.		

The second step is to ask at least two people that know you well and whose judgment you trust to answer the same questions about you. The people you ask can be friends, coworkers, or family members, as long as they have frequently observed how you behave in the types of situations described in the questionnaire. Conduct these informal interviews individually, and let the people you are asking know in advance what your purpose is; you need to be sure they are comfortable giving you feedback. It helps to preface your request with a statement like, "I want to improve my leadership skills, and I'm wondering if I can ask you a few questions about how you've seen me act in different situations. Please give me your honest feedback."

During the informal interviews, pose the questions and then write down the answers so that you can review them later. Don't argue with what you hear or respond in any way. It is natural to get emotional when we receive feedback—especially if that feedback is contrary to how we view ourselves. When we get emotional, we can't think clearly. So it is best to focus on writing down the feedback during the interview, then looking at it later, once your emotions have passed and you can process the information with a clear head.

When you review all the feedback from all your sources, you will probably see a consistent pattern in the responses to each question, favoring either task-oriented leadership or people-oriented leadership. This is how other people see your leadership style. If the feedback matches your self-assessment baseline, great. However, if the feedback you received is at odds with your baseline, I recommend favoring the feedback over your self-assessment.

Now that you know which skill category you tend to favor, *getting things done* or *focusing on people*, I'm going to make a recommendation that will probably seem counterintuitive: *consider starting your Leader Habit workout with an exercise from the opposite skill category.* Really.

If you tend to be a taskmaster, then you are most likely stronger in task-oriented leadership skills and you will have more opportunity for rapid improvement if you start by developing people-oriented skills, *so long as the skills you start with are generally compatible with your personality.* The same is true in reverse for people-focused leaders.

As you're thinking about this, don't overlook the caveat about picking a skill that is compatible with your personality. Your first exercise must be a behavior that comes to you naturally, feels easy, and that you intrinsically enjoy doing, so it needs to align with your personality traits. If you haven't done so already, go back and complete the exercise in Figure 3-1 in Chapter 3 or take the Leader Habit Quiz at www.leaderhabit.com to learn how you score on the six personality traits used by the Leader Habit Formula. (If you take the free online quiz, you will also receive a ranking of the top twenty-two leadership skills based on how they align with your personality. This can be a valuable tool to help you identify potential keystone habits.) Knowing your personality traits is essential to selecting the right exercise to start your Leader Habit workout.

At this point, you should have a good idea of which skill category you tend to be stronger in (*getting things done* or *focusing on people*), and you should know what your personality traits are. If you follow my recommendation, the best exercise to start your Leader Habit workout with is one that comes from your weaker skill category *and* aligns with your personality traits. So if you are a taskmaster, you would look for skills in *focusing on people* that also match your personality. To assist you in this, the catalogue of leadership skills and exercises in Part III describes the personality traits that influence each leadership skill. It's likely you will have several skills to choose from, depending on your traits. Generally speaking, if you score high on Caring and Outgoing, you will probably enjoy working on leadership skills that focus on people; if you score high on Organized and Ambitious, you will probably enjoy working on task-oriented leadership skills.

It is possible that your unique combination of personality traits will run counter to my recommendation. For example, you might be a taskmaster who scores low on Caring and Outgoing, meaning that people-oriented skills don't come naturally to you. My recommendation says your first exercise should be a people-oriented skill, but your personality traits suggest the opposite. This is not a problem. Remember that the most important thing about your *first* Leader Habit exercise is to choose one that is likely to become a keystone habit. This means you must enjoy doing it *and* it must build your self-efficacy—you need to get those early wins under your belt that make you believe you can be successful using the Leader Habit Formula. Starting with an exercise that doesn't align with your personality will be difficult because it won't feel easy or natural, it won't build your self-efficacy, and it probably won't become a keystone habit. So if my recommendation says to start with people-oriented skills but those skills are at odds with your personality, trust your personality and start your workout by practicing task-oriented skills instead. Yes, you're probably already strong on some of those skills, but in the early stages of your development it is more important to establish a keystone habit and build your self-efficacy than it is to work on your weaker skill category. Once you achieve those early wins and have confidence in your ability to grow, you can switch to the skills that feel less natural and require more effort to practice.

It's time to choose your first Leader Habit exercise. Take some time to look through the appropriate category in Part III. Find the skills that are most compatible with your personality traits and review the individual micro-behaviors and exercises for each of them. Ask yourself which exercise seems like it will be the easiest to start doing. Whichever one stands out to you, write it down and keep it close at hand. This is the exercise that will begin your leadership development workout.

If you have followed all my instructions up to this point and you're still having trouble selecting your first exercise, don't despair—sometimes even with feedback it's difficult to know exactly which leadership skill to start with. Narrowing the skills by category still leaves you with dozens of exercises to choose from. You might be tempted to just pick a skill from the list and hope for the best, but don't do that—it's better to play the odds than to guess at random. Based on the statistical analyses my team performed on the complete set of leadership skills, we identified the top three skills in each category that are most strongly related to the other skills in their respective domains; they are listed in Figure 5-2. When in doubt, start with one of these.

Figure 5-2 Most Likely Keystone Habits	
Getting Things Done	**Focusing on People**
The three leadership skills that are most strongly related to all other task-oriented behaviors are: 1. Create Urgency 2. Manage Priorities 3. Plan and Organize Work	The three leadership skills that are most strongly related to all other people-oriented behaviors are: 1. Influence Others 2. Overcome Individual Resistance 3. Mentor and Coach

Avoid the Trap of Individual Development Plans

A word of caution as you prepare for your Leader Habit workout: Don't fall into the trap of individual development plans. Many organizations around the world use development plans to document their employees' development goals by itemizing the skills they need to improve and the learning activities they should undertake. In theory this is an honorable effort, but in practice, at most organizations development plans have become just another bureaucratic exercise that consumes time and effort without producing the desired results. In fact, researchers at Maastricht University in the Netherlands found that, among 2,271 employees, those who had a development plan in place didn't plan to engage in more learning activities than non-users, nor did they see themselves as having stronger skills than non-users.[2] The only thing the employees with development plans were better at was creating development plans.

There are many reasons why development plans fail. Two in particular are worth highlighting in the context of the Leader Habit Formula. First, development plans are often too big. Spurred by the "more is better" fallacy, employees and managers cram too many learning activities into their plans, without regard for how much time those activities will require. The individual activities seem reasonable in isolation, but during busy workdays it is hard to find time to read a book, take a class, or practice a complex skill. As a result, employees struggle to make meaningful progress toward their development goals and soon those goals begin to feel overwhelming or impossible to achieve. And we have already seen what happens when people don't believe that they can do something—they procrastinate or give up.

The second reason why individual development plans fail is one we've already encountered; in fact, it's the same reason why most training and leadership development programs fail: They focus on acquisition of knowledge rather than skills and habits. As soon as someone says "learning activity," we're right back where we started with "read a book or take a class." The intentions are good, but, as we've already seen, the familiar methods and tools of knowledge-based instruction simply aren't effective at developing *skills*, which can only be done by practicing the behaviors that make up the skills we want to learn. It doesn't matter how many books you read about music theory or how many lectures you attend where someone explains proper piano-playing technique with glossy handouts and a slick PowerPoint presentation—*you can't learn to play the piano without actually playing the piano.* Similarly, you can read all the books you want on influence, empowerment, and coaching, but unless you start practicing those skills, you won't get better at them.

If you want your leadership development workout to succeed, don't waste time creating a big, overwhelming development plan—just start practicing your first Leader Habit exercise. After your self-efficacy increases and you start to believe that you can develop your leadership skills despite all of the inevitable distractions at work and at home, then you can think about putting together a long-term plan. For now, focus on turning your first exercise into a keystone habit, and the rest will follow.

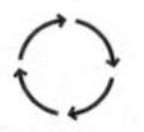

Understanding the Leader Habit Exercises

Before you start your workout, it's helpful to have a bit more background on the Leader Habit exercises. You already know that the exercises are simple by design, and no exercise should take more than five minutes to complete. The basic framework for each exercise is always the same: A cue is paired with a behavior that you do in response to the cue. The exercises vary in terms of when you perform them and what cue they are paired with.

There are three different types of exercises: *preparation exercises*, *just-in-time exercises*, and *reflection exercises*. As you can probably guess from the names, each type is distinguished by when it occurs relative to a given situation.

Preparation exercises are behaviors that are best done as you prepare for a specific event, like a meeting or a presentation. For example, one of the micro-behaviors for the skill Influence Others is anticipating how others will react to new ideas, plans, and initiatives. Since *anticipation* is by definition something you do in advance, this micro-behavior is ideally suited to a preparation exercise. For instance, before going into a meeting, you could write down one sentence describing how you think the person you are about to meet with will react to the topic you plan to discuss. Notice how simple and concrete the exercise is—it asks you to write something down and specifies exactly what to write.

Preparation exercises work well when the micro-behavior is more cognitive in nature—something that involves learning new patterns of thinking. In the previous example, the behavior was anticipating a reaction to plans. To make the process of anticipation more concrete and specific, the exercise asks you to write down one sentence. This is a common part of many of the exercises for cognitive tasks. Writing down what you think is a useful way to organize your thoughts, and it creates a tangible outcome from an abstract process.

Just-in-time exercises are practiced at the moment when the right situation presents itself. Just-in-time exercises almost always involve making statements or asking questions during interactions with other people. For example, to practice overcoming individual resistance, you could focus on finding two areas of agreement and summarizing each one as soon as you discover it by saying, "It seems to me that we agree on . . . Is that correct?" Laura's exercise of asking open-ended questions that start with the words "what" or "how" is another example of a just-in-time exercise.

Reflection exercises are practiced after an event has happened. Similar to preparation exercises, reflection exercises are best suited for cognitive tasks. For example, capitalizing on common interests and areas of agreement to build rapport is a micro-behavior for the skill Build Strategic Relationships. The exercise for this micro-behavior is practiced after a meeting or conversation has concluded and involves reflecting on two things that you have in common with the person, so that you can bring up those shared similarities in the next interaction. To make the reflection more concrete, you are asked to write those two things down.

As discussed in Chapter 2, the Leader Habit exercises are paired with natural cues—events that are embedded in the same context as the micro-behaviors you are practicing. Natural cues are better than artificial cues—for example, a sticky note on your computer or an alarm on your phone—because natural cues are always present in the situations where you are learning to apply your new behavior. A sticky note can fall off your computer and you can forget to set your alarm, and without these cues your new behavior will disappear. But what if your cue to reflect on the conversation you're having is the end of the conversation itself? That is universal to all conversations, and you never have to worry about "losing" your habit because its cue goes away.

Fortunately, the world is full of natural cues. The best natural cue is usually the end of a specific event or task. Recall one of the exercises for Influence Others: Before going into a meeting, you could write down one sentence describing how you think the person you are about to meet with will react to the topic you plan to discuss. This exercise has a natural cue built into it: *before going into a meeting*. But the built-in cue is not ideal because it is difficult to translate *before* into a specific time. If a meeting starts at 10:00 a.m., should you practice your exercise five minutes before the meeting? Ten minutes before? An hour before? Because the cue is vague, it will be difficult to recognize and remember. We need something more specific, preferably a cue tied to the end of an event that is related to the situation we are practicing for—in this case, an action that is usually performed right before going into a meeting and has a clear, concrete end. Is there such an action? Yes. Based on our observations, it turns out that most people check their calendar—they look up the name of the person they are meeting, the meeting location, or the conference line number. So a better natural cue for this exercise is: *after you check your calendar for your next meeting*—which is how you will find the exercise written in Part III. ("After-the-event" cues are easier to pair with reflection exercises because the reflection exercise itself happens after the event.)

Some cues are cognitive in nature—they cannot be observed by anyone else and happen in your head in the form of a decision, realization, or thought. These types of cues are good triggers for some of the just-in-time exercises, like asking for agreement on next steps at the end of a negotiation. Identifying a natural cue for this exercise involves figuring out when it is appropriate to do this behavior during a discussion, and what specific event or task naturally precedes the behavior. It turns out that, for many leaders, what triggers this behavior is the realization that the discussion is coming to an end. So the cue itself would be: *after you realize that the discussion is coming to an end*. Cognitive cues are most often used for just-in-time exercises, since these exercises must be practiced during specific events.

When you begin practicing an exercise, the connection between the behavior and the cue it is paired with will most likely be nonexistent. This is normal. Remember that you are creating the cue-behavior bond in your brain through deliberate practice. Each time you complete an exercise, those neurological connections are strengthened. With enough practice, you will progress with that behavior from weakness to proficiency to mastery to habit.

Track Your Practice

Now that you have settled on your first Leader Habit exercise, all you have to do is practice it for five minutes every day until it becomes a habit. Recall from Chapter 2 that it takes on average sixty-six days of practice for a behavior to turn into a habit.[3] For best results, I recommend tracking your progress, because it has been shown to help people achieve their goals.

Perhaps you know someone who has become obsessed with their pedometer and counting their steps every day. The premise is simple: If you track your steps, you are more likely to lose weight. But is it true?

Researchers at Unilever Corporate Research in the United Kingdom designed an experiment to test this question. They randomly assigned seventy-seven adults into two groups. Both groups received a wrist-worn device to monitor their activity level, but only one group had access to real-time tracking in the form of a smartphone application. After nine weeks, the researchers looked at how much physical activity each group logged during the period, and they measured changes in the participants' body fat.

The group that had access to the smartphone application (and therefore was able to track their progress) did much better than the control group in terms of both physical activity and change in body fat. On average, the tracking group logged two hours and eighteen minutes more physical activity than the control group (who didn't have access to the phone app and couldn't track their progress). Additionally, people in the tracking group lost more weight than people in the control group—on average 2 percent of their body fat.[4]

When it comes to your Leader Habit exercises, you are more likely to keep practicing if you record the days when you do it. There are many options available for this kind of tracking. You can use your calendar (paper or electronic) to mark the days when you practiced. You can set a recurring task on your smartphone or computer for the next sixty-six days. Or you can enter the exercise into a habit-tracking application like Streaks or Habit List. The method you choose is less important than the fact that you are tracking your progress. Each day you record your practice is another small victory in your ongoing leadership development workout. These small victories compound just like the successes that come from completing the exercise itself, and each small victory further increases your self-efficacy, making it easier to sustain your practice over time.

In the end, practice is the key. If you bought this book thinking you could improve your leadership skills just by reading it, I'm sorry to disappoint you. Reading this book won't make you a better leader unless you put the concepts into practice. So pick your first Leader Habit exercise, settle on a process to track your progress, and find five minutes today to start practicing. Applying the exercises in Part III to your everyday work and personal life will not only improve your leadership skills, but also teach you a more effective way to change your life and become the person you've always wanted to be—a great leader holding great habits.

PART III

EXERCISES THAT DEVELOP YOUR SKILLS

Here you will find the Leader Habit catalogue of the core leadership skills my team and I identified in our research and the 5-minute exercises we created for them. This catalogue is designed to be used as a reference for planning and executing your Leader Habit workout. Each skill includes:

- A definition of the skill and a breakdown of its specific micro-behaviors.
- A brief description of why the skill is important for effective leadership and how it influences your ability to achieve common business goals and strategy.
- A list of telltale signs that indicate you would benefit from improving the skill.
- A description of the personality traits aligned with the skill, to help identify what types of people will find the skill intrinsically rewarding.
- The 5-minute exercises that will help you develop the skill by turning its micro-behaviors into habits.

For guidance choosing your first Leader Habit exercise, refer back to Chapter 5: Starting Your Leader Habit Workout.

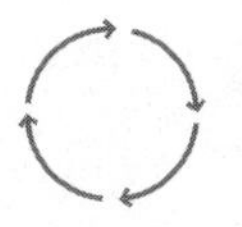

CHAPTER 6

Getting Things Done

Task-oriented leadership skills are about *getting things done.* Leaders with these skills are able to effectively keep people and teams on track, push for high performance, and help achieve organizational goals. They tend to initiate structure for their teams, plan and organize work, delegate well, monitor progress, and ensure that people get the job done. My research team and I identified eleven task-oriented leadership skills, which are grouped into three categories based on how the skills are conceptually related to each other. The three task-oriented categories are: Planning & Execution, Solving Problems & Making Decisions, and Leading Change.

Planning & Execution

Planning & Execution is a set of leadership skills that focus on proactively identifying what needs to be accomplished; splitting and delegating the work into projects, tasks, and assignments; and tracking and monitoring performance over time. These are rudimentary management skills that become especially important in leadership situations where you need to implement a new strategy, align teams with an existing strategy, improve products and services, increase accountability, implement new systems and processes, and improve efficiency of operations. There are four leadership skills in this category: Manage Priorities, Plan and Organize Work, Delegate Well, and Create Urgency.

SKILL: Manage Priorities

Managing priorities means identifying which tasks are most important and allocating appropriate time to accomplish them. In our research, we discovered the micro-behaviors that effective leaders do when they prioritize:

1. Break down the larger project into smaller tasks and assignments that are clear, concrete, and actionable, so that everyone knows exactly what to do.
2. Divide the tasks into more and less critical pursuits, e.g., identifying what needs to get done straightaway vs. what can wait until tomorrow.
3. Look at each task and assignment and estimate how long it will take to accomplish; the time estimates are realistic and comfortably achievable.
4. Base priorities on a solid, logical rationale, so that everyone understands why a particular task is more important than others.

WHY THE SKILL IS IMPORTANT FOR LEADERSHIP

You may feel like there always seems to be more work to be done than hours in the day, and that's why it's important to prioritize what is more and less critical to accomplish. Prioritizing enables you to focus your efforts on completing the tasks and projects that matter most. Without clear priorities, you will struggle to get anything done because everything will seem equally important and you won't know how to spend your time and energy most effectively. Similarly, when your team doesn't have clear priorities, individual members will struggle to coordinate their efforts effectively, they will feel overwhelmed by all the work coming their way, and the team will generally lack an understanding of what needs to be accomplished.

At work, managing priorities well is crucial to implementing a new strategy or aligning your team with an existing strategy. Implementation of any strategy involves translating the abstract strategy into concrete, actionable steps for people and teams to execute. If you cannot readily break down the strategy into smaller tasks or cannot prioritize such tasks, you will struggle to bring your team's activities and resources into line with the organization's planned objectives. The same is true for situations when you are charged with improving products and services, as such initiatives also rely on your ability to manage priorities.

TELLTALE SIGNS YOU NEED TO IMPROVE THIS SKILL

- If you feel overwhelmed with too many competing priorities.
- If you think that every task is equally important.
- If you can't manage your time well and miss deadlines as a result.
- If you cannot say "no" to people and often take on too much work.

PERSONALITY TRAITS ALIGNED WITH THIS SKILL

If you score *high on Organized and low on Curious,* you may find managing priorities intrinsically rewarding. If you are highly organized, you are probably methodical, systematic, and diligent; you enjoy planning. If you are low on Curious, you may be a more practical, concrete, linear thinker; you tend to be sensible and pragmatic. With this combination of traits, you are likely to derive satisfaction from behaviors like breaking down the larger project into clear, concrete steps; identifying smaller tasks and assignments; deciding which tasks are more critical than others; and estimating how long a task would take.

5-MINUTE LEADER HABIT EXERCISES

The following exercises will improve your ability to manage priorities.

Break down projects into tasks.

Although you probably won't start a new project every day, you can get in the habit of breaking down your daily tasks into smaller action items using this exercise: *After picking a task from your to-do list, write down two or three things you need to do to complete the task.* For example, if one of your tasks today is to create a presentation, your two action items could be to create the slides and then write the speaker notes.

Divide your tasks into more and less critical pursuits.

You can get in the habit of doing this behavior by starting your workday with this simple exercise: *After sitting down at your desk to start your workday, write down the two or three most important tasks you must complete that day.* Of course, you should work on these tasks before anything else.

Allocate appropriate time for completing your work.

This micro-behavior requires you to make an accurate estimate of how much time it will take you to complete a given task. Without accurate time estimates, it is difficult to plan your work and complete it on schedule. To turn this behavior into a habit, practice this exercise: *After adding a task to your to-do list, write down your estimate of how long it will take you to complete the task.* For example, you might estimate that it will take thirty minutes to draft an email informing your team about a new client project.

Be clear why something is a priority.

When prioritizing projects or tasks, make your rationale for the decision clear to yourself and others on your team. Use the following exercise to practice this micro-behavior on a daily basis: *After describing a project (in an email or a conversation), briefly explain why it is a priority by saying, "This is a priority because . . . ."* For example, you may prioritize a project because it is for your largest customer.

SKILL: Plan and Organize Work

Planning and organizing work means determining the resources needed to accomplish a given objective and planning who will do what by when. In our research, we discovered the micro-behaviors that effective leaders do when they plan and organize work:

1. Create a master project plan that specifies who will do what by when.
2. Identify the resources that will be needed during each phase of the plan, be they people, money, or materials.
3. Think creatively about how to use the available resources to stay within budget.
4. Put in place systems to track progress of individual contributors and teams, usually in the form of metrics and periodic check-ins.

WHY THE SKILL IS IMPORTANT FOR LEADERSHIP

As a leader, flawlessly executing a project requires strong planning and organizing skills on your part. Having a clear sense of who will do what and the resources they will need to do their work is critical for your success. Planning and organizing well enables you to effectively coordinate the efforts of multiple people and helps to ensure that everyone knows what is expected of them.

At work, planning and organizing skills are critical if you want to create accountability on your team and improve the efficiency of your company's operations. When you assign clear tasks and deadlines, you ensure that employees understand the scope and timelines of their work. When you track employees' progress with metrics and regular check-ins, you instill a sense of personal responsibility in each employee. Similarly, when you have a clear plan, you can better coordinate the efforts of your employees and teams, and so you cut out unnecessary productivity losses that result from faulty coordination.

TELLTALE SIGNS YOU NEED TO IMPROVE THIS SKILL

- If you scramble to get your work done at the very last minute.
- If you tend to cram the night before a big meeting.
- If your team members are confused about what to do and they don't complete their assignments on time.
- If your team lacks accountability.
- If your work lacks organization and clear structure.
- If it feels like you never have the resources needed to achieve your goals.

PERSONALITY TRAITS ALIGNED WITH THIS SKILL

If you score *high on Organized and high on Ambitious*, you may find planning and organizing intrinsically rewarding. If you are high on Organized, you are probably methodical, systematic, and diligent. If you are high on Ambitious, you may be confident and decisive; you enjoy putting structures in place and taking the initiative to plan for the future. With this combination of traits, you are likely to derive satisfaction from behaviors like putting a project plan together, identifying the resources you will need, and putting metrics in place to track progress.

5-MINUTE LEADER HABIT EXERCISES

The following exercises will improve your ability to plan and organize work.

Create a project plan.

Although you may not put together a full project plan every day, you can use this exercise to get in the habit of identifying tasks and setting deadlines: *After discussing a project or task with a coworker, identify one action item with a deadline by asking, "What exactly will you do and when will you complete it?" Write it down.* For example, your coworker commits to drafting a new product brochure by September 20.

Identify the resources you need.

This micro-behavior requires thinking about who or what you will need to complete a task. Use the following exercise to turn it into a habit: *After starting a task, write down two or three resources (people, money, materials) you need to get it done.* For example, if your task is to prepare a contract for a new client, you need someone from your legal team, the contract template, and your computer.

Use available resources creatively.

You can get in the habit of thinking creatively about using the resources you already have rather than wasting money on resources you think you need by practicing this exercise: *After you realize that you need a resource you don't currently have, ask yourself, "How can I use something I already have to achieve the same outcome?" Write down your answer.* For example, you could do a quick Internet search to learn how to create pivot tables in Excel rather than calling your IT help desk.

Track progress with metrics.

Get in the habit of tracking your own progress by practicing this exercise at the end of your workday: *After finishing your last task of the day, go through your to-do list and write down what percentage of each task you have completed.* For example, you may have completed 50 percent of your team meeting's agenda and 25 percent of your department's budget.

SKILL: Delegate Well

Delegating well means assigning projects that have a clear beginning and end and fit with the skills and interests of the person to whom you are delegating. In our research, we discovered the micro-behaviors that effective leaders do when they delegate well:

1. Think about the skill level of the person to whom the project is being delegated to determine if he or she has the ability to complete the project successfully.
2. Consider the person's interest to ensure that he or she will enjoy working on the project.
3. Identify what needs to be accomplished but let the person figure out how to accomplish it.

WHY THE SKILL IS IMPORTANT FOR LEADERSHIP

To be a successful leader, you must accept that you can't do everything yourself and learn to work through other people by delegating to them. When you delegate well, you will enable your team to achieve its goals quicker, produce better results, and accomplish much more than you ever could on your own, no matter how excellent and efficient you might be. Your team members will feel ownership of their projects and they won't feel like you are micromanaging them.

At work, if you don't delegate well you will struggle to retain your employees and keep them engaged, and your team's productivity will suffer. On one extreme, you may be hoarding all the projects for yourself and creating a bottleneck because everyone else has to wait for your input while you get overwhelmed with too much work. On the other extreme, you may be too eager to move projects off your plate and you end up overwhelming employees who don't yet have the skills to succeed with the work you give them. Leaders that micromanage or carelessly assign projects to unskilled or uninterested employees are difficult to work under. In these scenarios, employees tend to get disengaged and quit.

TELLTALE SIGNS YOU NEED TO IMPROVE THIS SKILL

- If you don't trust others to perform as well as you do.
- If you are overwhelmed with too many projects.
- If you end up checking every deliverable your team produces.
- If you assign projects that are too big for someone's skill level and they struggle.
- If you assign projects to people who don't really want them.

PERSONALITY TRAITS ALIGNED WITH THIS SKILL

If you score *high on Caring and low on Organized*, you may find delegating intrinsically rewarding. If you are high on Caring, you are probably perceptive, empathetic, and cooperative; you may enjoy empowering other people and supporting their efforts. If you are low on Organized, you are likely flexible and more tolerant of ambiguity. (In contrast, people who are too high on Organized may be rigid, controlling, perfectionistic, and risk-averse—characteristics that often result in micromanaging or refusing to delegate at all.) With the combination of high Caring and low Organized, you are likely to derive satisfaction from determining whether the person has the right skills to complete the project, considering the person's interests when deciding to delegate, and letting the person figure out how to complete the project.

5-MINUTE LEADER HABIT EXERCISES

The following exercises will improve your ability to delegate well.

Match projects to skills.

If the person to whom you are delegating isn't skilled enough to successfully complete the project, she will get overwhelmed and fail. If the person is too skilled, she will get bored and become disengaged. Effective delegation is about striking the right balance between giving someone too much of a challenge and not enough. You can get in the habit of assigning projects to people with the right skills by practicing this exercise: *After deciding to assign a project to a particular person, write down the two most important skills to get the job done and estimate the person's current skill level in those areas on a 1–5 scale.* For example, it takes planning and communication skills to organize a marketing event and the person might be a 3 on planning and a 4 on communication.

Match projects to interests.

If the person to whom you are delegating isn't interested in the project, they won't be motivated to complete it. To get in the habit of assigning projects that people want to do, practice this exercise: *After describing a project you wish to delegate, gauge the person's level of interest by asking, "Does this sound like something you'd be interested in?" Write down the response.* If the person you targeted is not interested, find someone else who might be a better fit.

Specify "what," not "how."

This micro-behavior is the opposite of micromanagement. Practice this exercise to get in the habit of letting others decide how they will do their work: *After deciding to delegate a project to a particular person, assign it by saying, "I'd like you to figure out how to. . . . How do you think you'll do that?" Write down the answer.* For example, you could say, "I'd like you to figure out how to collect customer feedback. How do you think you'll do that?" Make sure only to specify the end goal—the deliverable.

SKILL: Create Urgency

Creating urgency means setting bold and ambitious goals and building pressure on the team to accomplish them. In our research, we discovered the micro-behaviors that effective leaders do when they create urgency:

1. Set bold and audacious goals for self and others; these goals are achievable but provide a comfortable stretch for everyone.
2. Attach specific deadlines to projects and continuously stress the importance of achieving those results.
3. Communicate the urgency of projects and tasks in speech and emails with high-intensity words like "critical" and "crucial."

WHY THE SKILL IS IMPORTANT FOR LEADERSHIP

Creating urgency is an effective way to push individuals and teams to deliver results. Without a sense of urgency, your teammates won't push themselves to work hard, and they may procrastinate and struggle to get tasks and projects done on time. When people lack a sense of urgency, they are more easily sidetracked with daily distractions and can end up wasting time on tasks that are unimportant.

At work, you need to create urgency when you want to build a high-performance culture within a team or across an entire organization. A sense of urgency increases productivity and aligns your employees around the same ambitious goal. Your team members will develop their skills quicker when they are challenged to achieve bigger goals. Teams that feel a sense of urgency achieve superior business results.

TELLTALE SIGNS YOU NEED TO IMPROVE THIS SKILL

- If your teams often miss deadlines.
- If your employees get distracted with unimportant details.

- If you have a laid-back attitude about getting results.
- If you are afraid to set bigger, more ambitious goals.
- If your employees frequently procrastinate.

PERSONALITY TRAITS ALIGNED WITH THIS SKILL

If you score *high on Ambitious*, you may find creating urgency intrinsically rewarding. If you are high on Ambitious, you are likely driven to achieve goals and are often the boldest person in the room. You may be confident, decisive, energetic, persuasive, and influential. You may enjoy pushing for growth and initiating new projects. With this personality trait, you are likely to derive satisfaction from behaviors like setting bold and audacious goals, setting specific deadlines, and using high-intensity words.

5-MINUTE LEADER HABIT EXERCISES

The following exercises will contribute to your ability to create urgency.

Set bold goals.

If you shy away from bold goals, get in the habit of making small daily goals just a bit more ambitious with this exercise: *After starting your computer in the morning, write down one goal for the day by noting, "Today I will achieve. . . ." Then rewrite the goal to make it a bit more ambitious.* For example, if your goal today is to answer emails within three hours of receipt, you could make it a bit bolder by committing to answering emails within two hours and forty-five minutes. Then set a different goal tomorrow.

Stress the importance of results.

People work harder to meet deadlines when they believe the deadlines are important. This exercise will help you get in the habit of creating urgency around important deadlines: *After discussing an important task and its timeline, ask if it could be done sooner by saying, "This is crucial to our success. Could you get it done sooner?" Write down the reaction.*

Use high-intensity words.

You can gauge a person's sense of urgency not only by their actions and output (how much they get done) but also by the words they use to describe what they are doing. High-intensity words like "imperative," "critical," and "crucial" convey urgency and inspire it in others. Get in the habit of using high-intensity words with this exercise: After discussing an important task or project, emphasize its urgency with high-intensity words; for example, by saying, "Getting this done is absolutely critical!" Write down the phrase you used.

Solving Problems & Making Decisions

Solving Problems & Making Decisions is a set of leadership skills that focus on resolving issues through critical thinking. These skills are especially important in situations where you need to improve products and services for customers, implement new systems and processes, enhance efficiency of operations, increase profitability, and combine or restructure business units. There are four leadership skills in this category: Analyze Information, Think Through Solutions, Make Good Decisions, and Focus on Customers. The first three skills go together when solving a problem. First you have to fully understand what the problem is by collecting and integrating the relevant information (Analyze Information). Once you have a good understanding of the problem, you brainstorm multiple solutions, identify the advantages and disadvantages of each brainstormed solution, and set the criteria you will use to make the decision (Think Through Solutions). Then you make your decision by picking the most objective solution that addresses the underlying issue and is based on actions that follow logically from your analysis (Making Good Decisions). The last skill in this category (Focus on Customers) ensures that you take your customers' needs into account as part of your problem-solving and decision-making processes.

SKILL: Analyze Information

Analyzing information means collecting and integrating multiple pieces of data; researching a problem to understand it fully is the first step in an effective problem-solving process. In our research, we discovered the micro-behaviors that effective leaders do when they analyze information:

1. Review all available documents to find relevant information about the problem.
2. Integrate information from multiple sources to gain a novel insight, usually by comparing and contrasting different data points and sources and identifying the common theme that unites them.
3. Base decisions on multiple pieces of information and directly cite the different sources of evidence in support of the decision.

WHY THE SKILL IS IMPORTANT FOR LEADERSHIP

You can only solve a problem effectively if you understand its root cause, and you can only understand a problem's root cause through research and analysis. This means gathering data and taking the time to compare and contrast evidence from multiple sources, even when there is pressure to jump to quick conclusions. Without a good analysis, you cannot understand an issue properly, and you are likely to end up solving the wrong problem or just addressing superficial symptoms.

At work, strong analytical leadership is required to implement new systems and processes, improve efficiency of operations, or combine and restructure business units. When designing new workflow processes, you must first conduct an analysis (gather and evaluate information) to identify the underlying problems, redundancies, and opportunities for improvement. Similarly, when you are merging operations into a new entity or refocusing operations on core business activities, you will also need to conduct an analysis of workflows, interdependencies, and overlaps before you can design the new organizational structure.

TELLTALE SIGNS YOU NEED TO IMPROVE THIS SKILL

- If you make quick decisions without researching the problem.
- If you jump to conclusions based on limited information.
- If you have to go back often to solve the same problem all over again.
- If you find yourself solving the wrong problem.
- If you end up only patching up the surface symptoms and not addressing the root cause of the problem.

PERSONALITY TRAITS ALIGNED WITH THIS SKILL

If you score *high on Curious and high on Ambitious,* you may find analyzing information intrinsically rewarding. If you are high on Curious, you tend to be a creative, intellectual type; you enjoy contemplating ideas and solving complex problems. If you are high on Ambitious, you may be confident and decisive; you may have the drive and confidence to collect the necessary information and know when to stop. With this combination of traits, you are likely to derive satisfaction from behaviors like finding relevant information to the problem and integrating the different pieces of information to find common themes.

5-MINUTE LEADER HABIT EXERCISES

The following exercises will contribute to your ability to analyze information.

Research the issue.

You can get in the habit of reviewing available documents to find relevant information by double-checking decisions you make: *After you make a decision, consult one additional source (search the Internet or ask someone) and write down in one sentence how the new information supports or contradicts your decision.* For example, after deciding to give a customer discount, you may find out from your colleague that the same customer also received the same discount last week. If the new information contradicts your decision, go back and research the problem more.

Find the common theme.

You can gain a novel insight by comparing and contrasting the information you collected during your research and finding the common theme that unites the different data points. Practice this exercise: *After researching a problem, organize the information you have gathered in three to five bullet points and write down the common theme.* For example, you could find out that a few employees missed a deadline, others completed the wrong assignments, and yet others got in a heated conflict; the common theme here is the lack of coordination on the team.

Base decisions on multiple sources.

Practice this behavior by referencing the different sources you used to make your decision: *After stating your opinion (in an email or a meeting), give two pieces of evidence to support your position by saying, "I am basing this on . . . and . . . ."* For example, if you think that a meeting should be rescheduled, you could be basing it on several key people telling you they were unable to attend and the meeting agenda not being ready on time.

SKILL: Think Through Solutions

Thinking through solutions means carefully evaluating multiple solutions to a problem based on clear criteria; it is the second step in an effective problem-solving process. While analyzing information focuses on gaining an understating of the problem's root cause, thinking through solutions focuses on identifying and evaluating possible solutions to the problem. In our research, we discovered the micro-behaviors that effective leaders do when they think through solutions:

1. Brainstorm multiple solutions to the problem, not just one.
2. Identify advantages and disadvantages of solutions and critically evaluate their feasibility.
3. Identify the criteria you will use to select the best solution by clearly stating what the characteristics of the ideal solution are and what the solution needs to achieve.

WHY THE SKILL IS IMPORTANT FOR LEADERSHIP

Solving complex problems requires time, and it's unlikely that the first solution that comes to mind is the right one. That's why thinking through solutions is such an important leadership skill. As a leader, you face many problems on a daily basis, and it can be difficult to devote time and energy to finding the best solution to every problem, even when you have done your research. This skill enables you to consider all your options and ensures that you don't just settle on the first solution that comes to mind or make a reactive decision out of frustration. Such reactive decision-making often results in ineffective solutions that only address superficial issues and leave the underlying problems unresolved.

At work, thinking through solutions is important to the same leadership challenges as the skill Analyze Information: implementing new systems and processes, improving efficiency of operations, and combining and restructuring business units, just to name a few. After conducting a thorough analysis of a problem, you must generate many possible solutions and evaluate them against set criteria before deciding which is the best course of action; you cannot just go with the first solution that comes to mind. You have many options on how to redesign workflow processes or restructure business units, and each option has its advantages and limitations. As a leader, you need to be aware of your options and their shortcomings. Having a clear set of criteria of what constitutes the ideal solution will ensure that you select the right course of action for your people and teams.

TELLTALE SIGNS YOU NEED TO IMPROVE THIS SKILL

- If you get frustrated with problem-solving and just want the problem to disappear.
- If you don't consider the advantages and limitations of your decisions.
- If you feel the pressure to decide quickly.
- If you usually go with the first decision you can think of.
- If you have no idea about what the ideal solution should look like.

PERSONALITY TRAITS ALIGNED WITH THIS SKILL

If you score *high on Organized, high on Resilient, and high on Curious*, you may find thinking through solutions intrinsically rewarding. If you are high on Organized, you are probably methodical, systematic, and diligent; you enjoy thinking through before deciding. If you are high on Resilient, you are likely calm, even-tempered, and cool under pressure; you don't get easily frustrated or impatient while solving problems or feel the pressure to make a rash decision. If you are high on Curious, you tend to be creative and intellectual; you enjoy contemplating ideas and solving complex problems. With this combination of traits, you are likely to derive satisfaction from behaviors like brainstorming multiple solutions to the problem, thinking through advantages and disadvantages, and identifying criteria to select the best solution.

5-MINUTE LEADER HABIT EXERCISES

The following exercises will contribute to your ability to think through solutions.

Brainstorm multiple solutions.

Make a habit of considering multiple solutions by practicing this exercise: *After proposing a course of action (in an email or a meeting), list two alternatives you have considered by saying, "I settled on . . . after considering a few other options, such as . . . and . . . ." Write down the sentence.* For example, you may say, "I settled on weekly one-on-one check-ins after considering several options, such as team meetings and group training sessions."

Identify the advantages and disadvantages of a solution.

Make a habit of communicating to others that you have considered the limitations of a course of action, not just how it addresses the problem you are trying to solve: *After proposing an idea to someone, state one advantage and one limitation of your idea by saying, "I think that we should . . . ; it will help us with . . . , but it will not . . . ." Write down the sentence.* For example, you could say, "I think we should ask our employees how to improve our product; it will help us with their buy-in, but it will not get us customer feedback."

Define the ideal solution.

This micro-behavior requires having clear criteria for evaluating possible solutions to a problem. You can define the ideal solution by listing its different characteristics: *After realizing that you have a problem to solve, write down two or three bullet points of what the ideal solution should look like.* For example, "We need a plan that is easy to implement, accessible to everyone, and flexible in scope."

SKILL: Make Good Decisions

Making good decisions means understanding the underlying issues of the problem at hand and selecting a logical action that balances the needs of all involved parties; it is the final step in an effective problem-solving process. In our research, we discovered the micro-behaviors that effective leaders do when they make decisions:

1. Show full understanding of the problem and the root cause of the problem.

2. Select an objective course of action that meets the needs of each party involved and is not biased against any person or group.
3. Take an action that follows logically from the gathered information.
4. Avoid analysis paralysis by taking timely action even if not all information is present.

WHY THE SKILL IS IMPORTANT FOR LEADERSHIP

The world is full of complexity and there is rarely a perfect solution to any problem, but it is still possible to make good decisions. This skill builds on Analyze Information and Think Through Solutions. Leaders who make good decisions aren't impatient or reactive, and yet they don't overanalyze or delay their decisions unnecessarily. They do their research and consider many different options, and they don't let complexity or the temptation to find a perfect solution prevent them from taking action. By thinking through the limitations of different possible solutions, they ensure that their decisions balance the needs of the different parties involved. Good, confident decision-making leads teams in the right direction and prevents the false starts, detours, and second-guessing that can frustrate your followers and undermine morale.

At work, making good decisions is important to the same leadership challenges as the skills Analyze Information and Think Through Solutions: implementing new systems and processes, improving efficiency of operations, and combining and restructuring business units, just to name a few. After you conduct a thorough analysis of the problem and generate and evaluate multiple different solutions, you must pull the trigger and actually decide on a course of action. You cannot continue to collect and analyze data and generate possible solutions indefinitely. You need to pick the best solution in a timely manner and run with it. Similarly, you cannot keep changing your mind—once a decision is made, you need to implement it and move forward. Otherwise, you end up wasting time and resources.

TELLTALE SIGNS YOU NEED TO IMPROVE THIS SKILL

- If you fear making the wrong decision.
- If you feel like you need more data before you can decide.
- If you are waiting for the perfect solution to emerge.
- If you often change your mind.

PERSONALITY TRAITS ALIGNED WITH THIS SKILL

If you score *high on Ambitious, high on Organized, high on Resilient, and high on Curious*, you may find making good decisions intrinsically rewarding. If you are high on Ambitious, you are likely confident and decisive; you are not struck by decision paralysis and are comfortable with taking risks in decisions. If you score high on Organized, you are likely methodical, systematic, and diligent; you enjoy thinking through before deciding. If you are high on Resilient, you are likely calm, even-tempered, and cool under pressure; you don't get easily frustrated or impatient. If you are high on Curious, you tend to be creative and intellectual; you enjoy contemplating ideas and solving complex problems. This is why you can derive satisfaction from behaviors like discovering the underlying issues, finding an objective decision that balances the needs of all parties, and making a timely decision even if not all of the information is present.

5-MINUTE LEADER HABIT EXERCISES

The following exercises will contribute to your ability to make good decisions.

Show that you understand the underlying issues.

Most problems consist of several visible symptoms caused by a hidden underlying problem, or root cause. The best decisions address root causes, but first you must identify these causes by digging deeper into the nature of the problem you are trying to solve. Practice this exercise:

After learning about a problem, ask yourself, "What's the root cause here?" Write down your answer. For example, two of your employees have gotten into an argument about an upcoming deadline. The deadline is the superficial problem, but you identify that the root cause is a lack of trust between these two individuals.

Select an objective course of action.

There is always a risk that a decision will inadvertently disadvantage a person or group involved in a situation. Good decisions avoid this risk by ensuring that a course of action is objective and fair to all parties involved. Make this a habit by practicing the following exercise: *After deciding on a course of action, ask yourself, "Who could this action negatively impact and what would that impact be?" Write down your answer.* For example, you could decide to implement a work-from-home policy for your team that could negatively impact employees with small children, because those children could be a distraction.

Explain your rationale.

Once you have completed your analysis and identified your solution, it is time to act. Show everyone that you are making a logical decision by explaining your rationale using this exercise: *After you recommend a course of action, explain your rationale behind it by saying, "We should do . . . because . . . ." Write it down.* For example, you could recommend delaying a product release by saying, "We should delay releasing the product because our initial tests revealed many serious bugs. Releasing a buggy product could harm our reputation in the market."

Take timely action even if not all information is present.

Don't put off making a decision so you can collect more data in the hope of finding the perfect solution. If you fear making a mistake or feel uncomfortable making the big decision, think of it as making a series of smaller decisions instead: *After noticing that you want to do more research to collect additional data, ask yourself, "What small decision can I make today?" Write it down.* For example, if deciding on your entire annual budget feels overwhelming and you find yourself wanting to collect more information from your colleagues instead of finalizing the budget, you could think of it as making a series of four smaller decisions, and today you can decide on just your budget for the first quarter.

SKILL: Focus on Customers

Focusing on customers means understanding your customers' needs and bringing those needs to the forefront of your decision-making process. In our research, we discovered the micro-behaviors that effective leaders do when they focus on customers:

1. Clearly define who your customers are.
2. Seek information about and anticipate your customers' current and future needs by explicitly asking questions to learn more about those needs and stressing the importance of customer feedback in oral and written communication.
3. Base decisions on customer feedback by making decisions that explicitly incorporate themes from customer feedback and cite the customer feedback as rationale for the decision.
4. Set high standards of customer service and clearly communicate expectations for appropriate behavior toward customers.

WHY THE SKILL IS IMPORTANT FOR LEADERSHIP

As a leader, you will often be called upon to address day-to-day operational issues and emergencies, such as interpersonal conflicts, lack of resources, or unreasonable timelines. Because of their immediacy, it is easy for these types of issues to distract you from your organization's customers. As important as operational issues and emergencies are, your customers are more so—they are the reason your organization exists in the first place. To be an effective leader, you must always remember who your decisions impact the most—your customers—and give their needs ample consideration in your day-to-day work. After all, your customer should come first!

At work, focusing on customers will enable you to enhance your company's customer value proposition, increase customer satisfaction, better differentiate products and services from competitors, strengthen your company's brand and reputation, and increase customer loyalty. The more you focus on your customers, the better you will understand who they are and what their current needs are, and you will be able to anticipate their future needs. You will consider how your decisions impact your customers and ensure that your teams provide high levels of customer service. Through these behaviors, you can increase the benefits customers receive by purchasing your products and services, and you can improve all interactions with customers at the time of sale and thereafter to exceed customers' expectations.

TELLTALE SIGNS THAT YOU NEED TO IMPROVE THIS SKILL

- If you don't think of the customer when making decisions.
- If you are unclear who your customers are.
- If your customers don't return to purchase more.
- If you think that you already know what your customers need and want.
- If your customers are often dissatisfied with your product or service.
- If you don't think about your customers at least once per day.

PERSONALITY TRAITS ALIGNED WITH THIS SKILL

If you score *high on Caring and high on Curious*, you may find focusing on customers intrinsically rewarding. If you are high on Caring, you are likely perceptive, supportive, and empathetic; you are good at reading people's needs and go out of your way to ensure that they are pleased. If you are high on Curious, you are likely a strong strategist and visionary; you enjoy solving complex problems and strategizing different business scenarios. With this combination of traits, you are likely to derive satisfaction from behaviors like providing high levels of customer care, learning about what your customers desire, and bringing customer feedback into your decision-making.

5-MINUTE LEADER HABIT EXERCISES

The following exercises will contribute to your ability to focus on customers.

Define your customers.

Let everyone know how you define your customer base in concrete terms. Make it a habit to regularly reference this definition during daily meetings and in email: *After discussing an internal operations problem, remind your team that you're ultimately solving the problem for your customers by saying, "This is ultimately a solution for [define the customer]; they're our top priority."* For example, a school principal may say: "This is ultimately a solution for the parents and students at this school; they're our top priority."

Study the needs of your customers.

Learn what your customers want now and anticipate what they'll want in the future by practicing this exercise: *After finishing lunch, spend five minutes researching customer demand trends by reading an industry report or a customer survey. Write down one thing you learned.* For example, you might learn that your customers now take shorter vacations that only last a few days rather than the weeks-long vacations they took in the past.

Base decisions on customer feedback.

This micro-behavior is about incorporating customer feedback directly into your daily decision-making process: *After realizing you need to make a decision, ask yourself, "What customer feedback can I incorporate into this decision?" Write down your answer.* For example, if you must decide where to outsource production and your customers have said that they appreciate European designs, you might consider moving production to central or eastern Europe rather than China.

Expect high standards of customer service.

Make it a point to emphasize what you consider appropriate behavior toward customers in everyday interactions by practicing this exercise: *After discussing the last agenda item in a meeting, reiterate how you expect employees to behave toward customers by saying, "I expect that you . . . ." Write it down.* For example, a manager who oversees an IT help desk might say, "I expect that you are patient with the people we support, resolve their issues quickly, and make them feel valued."

Leading Change

Leading Change is a set of leadership skills that focus on instigating change and bringing everyone on board to make the change happen in the organization. These skills are especially important in situations when you need to boost innovation, build a culture of continuous improvement, implement new organizational strategy, or refocus the organization on new markets. There are three leadership skills in this category: Sell the Vision, Innovate, and Manage Risk. The last two skills are opposites on the same spectrum—some leaders tend to be risk-averse, which prevents them from innovating at all, while others tend to innovate recklessly, which exposes their organizations to unnecessary risks.

SKILL: Sell the Vision

Selling the vision means inspiring others with your organization's vision and convincing them to embrace it. In our research, we discovered the micro-behaviors that effective leaders do when they sell the vision:

1. Paint a vivid picture of the organization's future state, so that the audience can envision the arrival point (think "man on the moon").
2. Communicate specific long-term goals that span three to five years.
3. Make the vision relevant to your followers by appealing to their personal values and needs.

WHY THE SKILL IS IMPORTANT FOR LEADERSHIP

Having a clear sense of where the organization is going motivates people to work harder and gives them a direction so they understand what's more and less critical. This is especially true when you are implementing change. Change creates uncertainty and resistance. People are more likely to accept change when you present a clear vision for the future that is vivid, compelling, easy to understand and remember, and personally relevant.

At work, selling the vision is important to leadership challenges that require you to establish a strategic direction, launch a start-up or build new products and services, or implement a new organizational strategy. You must have clear goals and vision before you can determine the long-term direction and scope of your organization. Similarly, if you're launching a new organization, business unit, or products and services, then everyone on your team must have a solid understanding of the new direction before they can make it a reality.

TELLTALE SIGNS YOU NEED TO IMPROVE THIS SKILL

- If you see strategic planning and visioning as an impractical and useless exercise.

- If vision and long-term goals are just unfounded speculations to you.
- If you don't want to commit to any long-term goals because you fear not reaching them.
- If you can't summarize the vision of your organization in one sentence.
- If your followers don't understand how the organization's goals benefit them personally.

PERSONALITY TRAITS ALIGNED WITH THIS SKILL

If you score *high on Ambitious and high on Outgoing*, you may find selling the vision intrinsically rewarding. If you are high on Ambitious, you are likely confident, energetic, persuasive, and influential; you enjoy initiating new projects, pushing for growth, and providing thoughts and plans about the future. If you are high on Outgoing, you are likely charming, talkative, dynamic, and enthusiastic; you like to express excitement and compel others to action. With this combination of traits, you are likely to derive satisfaction from behaviors like painting a picture of the organization's future, setting long-term goals, and appealing to followers' personal values and needs.

5-MINUTE LEADER HABIT EXERCISES

The following exercises will contribute to your ability to sell the vision.

Paint a vivid picture.

To practice this micro-behavior on a daily basis, picture the arrival point or end state of a task when you ask people to do something—what visible sign would tell you that the person had completed the task? The following exercise will help you turn this visualization technique into a habit: *After asking someone to do a task, describe the very first sign you would need to see in order to conclude that the task has been completed by saying,*

"When it's done, it will look like . . . ." For example, if I asked you to order supplies, I would know that you did it after seeing a fully stocked supply cabinet.

Think long term (three to five years).

Generally speaking, organizational goals span three to five years. You probably won't create multiyear goals every day, but you can practice long-term thinking by applying it to your everyday projects: *After discussing a project (in an email or a meeting), state how it will be different in three to five years by saying, "In three to five years, we will probably . . . ."* For example, when discussing plans for a new website, you could say, "In three to five years, we will probably have all customizations incorporated into the online buying experience, so that customers can purchase fully customized products without ever interacting with our reps."

Make the vision personally relevant.

This micro-behavior involves translating the vision into something that followers personally value and want—something that is a clear benefit to them. Get in the habit of making projects, tasks, and ideas personally relevant for people by practicing this exercise: *After pitching a new project or idea, highlight how it's personally relevant for them by saying, "The personal benefits to you are . . . ."* For example, after asking a salesperson to write a blog for the company, you could say, "The personal benefits to you are gaining visibility on the company website and social media and building your personal brand as a thought leader."

SKILL: Innovate

Innovating means proposing creative solutions to important problems. In our research, we discovered the micro-behaviors that effective leaders do when they innovate:

1. Think "outside the box" by taking a holistic approach to combine seemingly unrelated ideas; see the connections between information that others don't see.
2. Brainstorm creative solutions to problems; the solutions are novel, unique, and unexpected.
3. Celebrate and encourage experimentation and calculated risk-taking; inspire others to try something new.
4. Focus innovative efforts on problems that are meaningful and pressing rather than innovating for the sake of innovation.

WHY THE SKILL IS IMPORTANT FOR LEADERSHIP

There is always room for improvement, whether that means better serving your customers, building a better product, or better coordinating efforts on your team. That's what innovation is: doing things better. Leaders who innovate well give their organizations a competitive advantage by creating products and services that stand apart from the competition. Furthermore, they foster innovation in others by supporting creative ideas, thinking strategically, and challenging the status quo.

At work, your innovative leadership will support a culture of experimentation and continuous improvement and inspire your teams to be more creative. You will create and maintain a competitive advantage for your company by encouraging advancements in products and services and day-to-day business operation.

TELLTALE SIGNS YOU NEED TO IMPROVE THIS SKILL

- If you don't want things to change.
- If you only see the risks in doing things differently.
- If you ask, "What's wrong with how we do things now?" when confronted with change.
- If you always solve problems in the same way.

- If you can't picture what a creative solution to a problem would look like.

PERSONALITY TRAITS ALIGNED WITH THIS SKILL

If you score *high on Curious and low on Organized*, you may find innovating intrinsically rewarding. If you are high on Curious, you tend to be a creative type and you enjoy offering suggestions about new and different ways of doing things, discussing new ideas, encouraging others to think along new lines, and experimenting with new approaches. If you are low on Organized, you are likely flexible and more tolerant of ambiguity, which are prerequisites to creativity. (In contrast, people who are high on Organized tend to be risk-averse, rigidly adherent to the status quo, and resistant to change, qualities that make innovation difficult for them.) With the combination of high on Curious and low on Organized, you are likely to derive satisfaction from behaviors like brainstorming creative solutions or encouraging others to experiment with new approaches.

5-MINUTE LEADER HABIT EXERCISES

The following exercises will contribute to your ability to innovate.

Combine seemingly unrelated ideas.

Creative insight usually comes when you discover the commonality between two things that at first appear to be unrelated. To get in the habit of thinking outside the box, practice this exercise: *After you or someone else uses the word "but" when describing two opposite ideas, ask, "How are these two things connected?" Write down the answer.* For example, someone could say, "Most customers love our product, but there are some who hate it," and the connection between the two apparent opposites is that all customers have a strong emotional reaction to your product.

Brainstorming creative solutions.

In the context of this exercise, creativity means solving a problem in an unconventional way—in other words, not using the established process that most people utilize. On a daily basis you could practice brainstorming creative solutions by imagining that you had an unlimited budget for solving problems: *After learning about a problem, ask yourself, "How would I solve this problem if I had all the money in the world?" Write down one idea.* For example, you could realize that to serve your customers better, you need to create a new prototype team that will test and document new solutions before rolling them out to all your clients.

Celebrate experimentation.

You can get in the habit of inspiring others to try a new approach and learn from it. Practice this exercise: *After someone proposes a new idea, ask, "What would it take to try this?" Write down the answer.* After hearing the details, you may decide to pilot-test the new idea.

Focus creative efforts on meaningful problems.

Creative thinking is wasted effort if it doesn't produce solutions to important problems. This exercise will help you get in the habit of focusing innovation on things that matter: *After coming up with a new idea, ask yourself, "How is this addressing our most important problem?" Write down the answer.* For example, you may propose to rent out a portion of an office building your company owns, and the additional income could address your company's problem of seasonal cash flow inconsistency by providing a new source of stable revenue.

SKILL: Manage Risk

Managing risk means anticipating threats from multiple areas and creating contingency plans to address them. In our research, we discovered the micro-behaviors that effective leaders do when they manage risk:

1. Anticipate threats from multiple areas; brainstorm different scenarios of things going wrong.
2. Include pilot-testing and feedback loops as part of innovation; test new ideas before implementing them and create ways to monitor the progress of implementations.
3. Develop contingency plans to handle errors and failures; always have a Plan B ready to go.

WHY THE SKILL IS IMPORTANT FOR LEADERSHIP

It is possible to have too much of a good thing—even innovation and ambition. Constantly pursuing new solutions and big goals can lead to reckless decisions that increase risk. The possible consequences of recklessness and excessive risk include decreased customer satisfaction and brand loyalty, financial losses, and harm to your reputation. Managing risk responsibly is therefore crucial to your success. Innovators can sometimes become "addicted" to change and novelty, rushing to implement every new and shiny fad without considering its long-term risk to the organization. Others may be too aggressive in their pursuit of success and set overly ambitious goals that are far removed from reality and simply cannot be achieved.

At work, managing risk is especially important with your entrepreneurial endeavors like launching a start-up (a new organization or division), building new products and services, or entering new markets. There is a fine line between entrepreneurial risk-taking and recklessness. Some business opportunities you encounter are riskier than others, and you must have the skill to anticipate and effectively manage such risks.

TELLTALE SIGNS YOU NEED TO IMPROVE THIS SKILL

- If you want to change things around just for the sake of change.
- If new and shiny things excite you and you must have them.
- If your goals are really big and bold but seldom achievable.

- If you don't pilot-test your ideas and go straight to implementation.
- If you don't believe in having a Plan B.

PERSONALITY TRAITS ALIGNED WITH THIS SKILL

If you score *high on Organized and low on Ambitious*, you may find managing risk intrinsically rewarding. If you are high on Organized, you are likely conservative, reliable, dependable, and diligent (but if you are very high on Organized, you may tend toward risk-aversion). If you are low on Ambitious, you are likely laid-back, unhurried, and reluctant to take charge. With this combination of personality traits, you are probably not prone to risky decisions, and so you are likely to derive satisfaction from behaviors like anticipating risks, pilot-testing ideas, and developing contingency plans.

5-MINUTE LEADER HABIT EXERCISES

The following exercises will contribute to your ability to manage risk.

Anticipate threats from multiple areas.

Risks can come from anywhere—internal operations, changes in customer demand, innovations in the supply chain, disruptive technologies, and shifts in the global economy, just to name a few. Practice this exercise on a daily basis to get in the habit of anticipating them: *After making a decision, ask yourself, "What changes in operations, customers, or the economy could pose a threat to my decision?" Write down your answer.* For example, if you decide to invest in expanding the parking lots for your retail stores, increases in global fuel prices could pose a threat to your decision because not as many of your customers would drive to your stores.

Pilot-test your ideas.

Before you decide to implement any new idea, pilot-test it to understand how it will work in practice: *After coming up with an idea, identify one low-risk way to pilot-test its viability. Write down your idea.* For example, if you come up with an idea to enhance your product, create a mock-up of it first and present it to a few trusted customers before making a large investment.

Have a Plan B.

Get in the habit of developing contingency plans to handle errors and failures by practicing this exercise: *After coming up with a solution to a problem, ask yourself, "What will I do if my solution doesn't work?" Write down your Plan B.* For example, if you plan to host an online videoconference, your Plan B might be a backup telephone bridge in case someone loses Internet access.

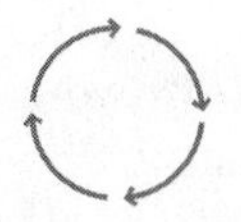

CHAPTER 7

Focusing on People

People-oriented leadership skills are about keeping others engaged, motivated, and satisfied. Leaders with these skills support their followers by building and maintaining relationships. They tend to be charismatic and have strong interpersonal skills that help them to effectively motivate and influence people, and they actively help others grow and develop. My research team and I identified eleven people-oriented leadership skills, which are grouped into three categories: Persuasion & Influence, Growing People & Teams, and Interpersonal Skills.

Persuasion & Influence

Persuasion & Influence is a category of leadership skills that focus on motivating people to achieve organizational goals. As a leader, you work through others, and that means you need the skills to persuade and influence them to get the work done. These leadership skills are especially important in situations when you need to achieve goals like aligning teams with organizational strategy; combining or restructuring business units; and building strategic alliances with suppliers, vendors, and partners. There are three leadership skills in this category: Influence Others, Overcome Individual Resistance, and Negotiate Well.

SKILL: Influence Others

Influencing others means affecting others' thinking and behavior by uncovering concerns and presenting convincing arguments. In our research, we discovered the micro-behaviors that effective leaders do when they influence others:

1. Anticipate how others will react to new ideas, plans, and initiatives.
2. Ask targeted questions to explore people's concerns.
3. Skillfully guide the discussion away from surface issues to underlying concerns to ensure that you are addressing root causes, not just symptoms.
4. Uncover hidden requests so you can accurately and fully address people's needs.

WHY THE SKILL IS IMPORTANT FOR LEADERSHIP

Contrary to popular belief, most formal leadership positions come with only a limited amount of influence. Sure, you can take an authoritarian stance and order people around and in general it will result in compliance, but compliance is not commitment. People will perform the tasks you tell them to, but you won't get their best efforts. As a leader, your job is to motivate people to want to do their tasks because they believe that what you are asking them to do is the right course of action. Therefore it is important for you to anticipate how people will react to new plans, ideas, and initiatives; to hear and understand their concerns; and to address those concerns effectively. When people feel they are being heard, and when they know you have considered their points of view, they are more likely to get on board with what you are asking. To get things done, you must achieve more than mere compliance. You must get people to believe in your ideas and initiatives and commit to making them happen.

At work, getting your followers on board is crucial to aligning teams with organizational strategy, implementing new systems and processes, and combining and restructuring business units. If you cannot effectively use influence tactics, you will struggle to lead these types of change efforts specifically, and in general you will find it difficult to motivate people to do what needs to be done.

TELLTALE SIGNS YOU NEED TO IMPROVE THIS SKILL

- If you struggle to motivate people to do what needs to be done.
- If you expect people to complete tasks just because you tell them to do so.
- If you are surprised by people's negative reaction to your plans.
- If people resist the changes you are trying to make.
- If you cannot convince people that your way is the right way.

PERSONALITY TRAITS ALIGNED WITH THIS SKILL

If you score *high on Ambitious and high on Resilient,* you may find influencing others intrinsically rewarding. If you are high on Ambitious, you are probably confident and persuasive; you enjoy influencing other people. If you are high on Resilient, you are probably calm, even-tempered, and cool under pressure; you don't get impatient and easily frustrated. With this combination of traits, you are likely to derive satisfaction from behaviors like anticipating people's reactions to plans, exploring others' concerns, and presenting solid arguments.

5-MINUTE LEADER HABIT EXERCISES

The following exercises will improve your ability to influence others.

Anticipate reactions.

People don't always react to new ideas positively, especially if those ideas have a direct impact on their work and personal lives. You can prepare a better influence strategy if you anticipate how people will react. Practice this exercise to make a habit of it: *After checking your calendar for your next meeting, write down one sentence describing how you think the person you are about to meet with will react to the topic you plan to discuss.* For example, if you plan to discuss an idea for the new company logo, you could write down, "I think Suzy will like the colors but she may not like the shape."

Ask about concerns.

People are more likely to get on board with new ideas and new ways of doing things when they feel their concerns are being heard. Use this exercise to practice asking questions that target people's concerns: *After someone expresses a concern or dissatisfaction (in an email or meeting), ask a targeted question to better understand the person's position by saying, "What makes you concerned about this?"* For example, if someone on your team is unhappy about the online meeting software your company uses, you could better understand her concerns by asking, "What makes you concerned about the software we use?"

Guide the discussion toward root causes.

Oftentimes people's concerns come from their misunderstanding of the problem they face. You can get in the habit of helping people identify the root cause of their concerns by practicing this exercise: *After someone describes a problem to you, acknowledge the problem and ask about the underlying issue by saying, "I understand that . . . is a problem, but I wonder if it could be a symptom of a different underlying issue we should discuss."* For example, if someone complains about his coworker being unreliable and missing deadlines, the underlying issue could be that the person missing deadlines took on too many tasks and is overwhelmed.

Uncover and address the hidden request.

When people complain about something, there is usually a request hidden within the complaint. If you uncover what the hidden need is, you can meet it with a solid, logical solution. Practice this exercise: *After hearing someone complain, ask what his or her hidden request is by saying, "Thank you for voicing your concerns. What is it that you are requesting?"* For example, if customers complain about being charged late fees, they are probably requesting that you waive those fees.

SKILL: Overcome Individual Resistance

Overcoming individual resistance means eliminating people's reluctance to change by addressing their fears and objections and convincing them to take action. In our research, we discovered the micro-behaviors that effective leaders do when they overcome resistance:

1. Explicitly address people's fears and reluctance by acknowledging their negative emotions and helping them to name those emotions.
2. Sell people on the benefits of change by highlighting how they will personally benefit from the change.
3. Facilitate the discussion to mutual agreement; periodically check the understanding of all parties involved and summarize what has been agreed on so far during the discussion.
4. Convince people to take action by highlighting shared goals.

WHY THE SKILL IS IMPORTANT FOR LEADERSHIP

Change is never easy. People tend to avoid it whenever they can and resist it when they can't. Any of your requests that people do things differently has the potential to be met with resistance, either passive or active. As a leader, you need to understand where the resistance is coming from, address any strong emotions head-on, and focus on finding common ground. Resistance usually comes from a place of fear and uncertainty. The resistant individual is not trying to be difficult or make your day miserable; he or she is simply scared of the unknown and needs reassurance that you are on his or her side.

At work, you must be skilled at overcoming resistance in order to effectively align teams with organizational strategy, increase customer satisfaction, and implement new systems and processes. If you don't address sources of resistance early on and show people that you're on their side, their negativity can spread. What started as a single resistant individual can grow into an entire resistance movement in the organization and undermine your ability to achieve organizational goals.

TELLTALE SIGNS YOU NEED TO IMPROVE THIS SKILL

- ▸ If people openly resist your plans and ideas.
- ▸ If you are not aware of or sympathetic to people's fears and insecurities.
- ▸ If you cannot readily articulate how someone's life will be better after the change.
- ▸ If it seems like you cannot come to an agreement with a particular person.
- ▸ If you cannot convince someone to act differently.
- ▸ If you cannot identify what you have in common with the resistant person.

PERSONALITY TRAITS ALIGNED WITH THIS SKILL

If you score *high on Ambitious, high on Outgoing, and high on Resilient,* you may find overcoming individual resistance intrinsically rewarding. If you are high on Ambitious, you are probably confident and persuasive; you enjoy influencing other people. If you are high on Outgoing, you are probably charming, talkative, and enthusiastic; you build rapport quickly. If you are high on Resilient, you are probably calm, even-tempered, and cool under pressure; you don't get impatient and easily frustrated. With this combination of traits, you are likely to derive satisfaction from behaviors like addressing people's fears, selling them on the benefits of change, reaching an agreement, and convincing people to take action.

5-MINUTE LEADER HABIT EXERCISES

The following exercises will improve your ability to overcome individual resistance.

Address fears.

Resistance usually comes from strong negative emotions, such as when people feel threatened by change or fearful of it. Acknowledging these negative emotions and helping people to name them is an effective way to overcome resistance. Get in the habit of asking about people's fears and reluctance using this exercise: *After noticing even the slightest resistance, ask a question to learn about the person's concerns by saying, "Can you tell me what about this may not feel right to you?"* For example, a colleague may show slight resistance in the form of an "I agree with you, but . . ." statement, and you could ask, "Can you tell me what about this doesn't feel right to you?"

Highlight benefits of change.

On the rational level, resistance may also come from misunderstanding the change or from a lack of awareness of its benefits. You can practice selling individuals on the benefits of change using this exercise: *After identifying a procedure that you need to change, ask yourself, "How will people benefit from changing this workflow?" Write it down in one sentence.* For example, the benefit of streamlining your quality assurance process would be that employees have fewer checklists to fill out, resulting in less required overtime.

Find two areas of agreement.

This micro-behavior requires making a conscious effort to periodically summarize areas of agreement during a discussion, which demonstrates to the other person that you are on his side, not his enemy. Practice this exercise: *After starting a conversation, focus on finding two areas of agreement. Summarize each one as soon as you discover it by saying, "It seems to me that we agree on . . . ; is that correct?"* For example, you could agree that you are both committed to addressing the issue under discussion, and you both want to reach a mutually agreeable solution to the problem.

Identify and highlight shared goals.

It is easier to overcome resistance if you can convince people that an action is linked with their goals. Use this exercise to practice identifying shared goals: *After finishing a meeting, write down one goal that you share with the other people involved in the meeting.* For example, your shared goal could be to have a smooth product launch, or to satisfy your customers.

SKILL: Negotiate Well

Negotiating well means engaging in bargaining discussions that achieve win-win agreements. In our research, we discovered the micro-behaviors that effective leaders do when they negotiate:

1. Communicate your intention to find a win-win solution and focus on understanding the other party's main concerns.
2. Engage in collaborative problem-solving; deliberately incorporate goals, ideas, and information from both parties into the discussion.
3. Explain how the preferred solution adds value and describe its positive impact.

4. Specify next steps and explicitly ask for agreement on those steps.

WHY THE SKILL IS IMPORTANT FOR LEADERSHIP

As a leader, you are probably involved in negotiations on a daily basis, even if you don't realize it: Any time you attempt to reach an agreement with another party through dialogue, you are negotiating. Sometimes your negotiations are formal, like negotiating a contract with a client or a new company policy. Other times, your negotiations are informal, such as resolving a conflict with a team or a coworker. Regardless, all negotiations are interpersonal interactions, which means they are fundamentally about relationships. Depending on how you handle the situation, a negotiation can either harm the underlying relationship or strengthen it. If you negotiate well and achieve an outcome that benefits both parties, you will build trust and improve your relationship with the other party. But if you push to come out of the negotiation as the winner at the other party's expense, you will harm the relationship.

Although negotiation skills are important for every leader, they are especially important when your goal is to build strategic alliances with suppliers, vendors, or partners. You need strong negotiating skills to establish mutually beneficial relationships with other firms and entities to pursue common business goals. Similarly, strong negotiation skills are important in merger and acquisition deals when your goal is to expand the business through merged operations and new entities.

TELLTALE SIGNS YOU NEED TO IMPROVE THIS SKILL

- If you see negotiations as a game and you feel like you have to win even if others lose.
- If you walk away from negotiations feeling like you got the short end of the stick.

- If you get afraid during negotiating that you may lose too much and you just give in.
- If you are uncomfortable taking a tough stance to defend your position.
- If negotiations stress you out and you actively avoid them.
- If you spend more time talking than listening during negotiations.

PERSONALITY TRAITS ALIGNED WITH THIS SKILL

If you score *high on Ambitious, low on Outgoing, and high on Resilient,* you may find negotiating intrinsically rewarding. If you are high on Ambitious, you are probably confident, decisive, energetic, persuasive, and influential; you enjoy negotiating. If you are low on Outgoing, you are probably composed and reserved; you enjoy listening to people. If you are high on Resilient, you are probably calm, even-tempered, and cool under pressure; you don't get impatient and easily frustrated. With this combination of traits, you are likely to derive satisfaction from behaviors like finding a win-win solution, collaboratively solving problems, and reaching an agreement on next steps.

5-MINUTE LEADER HABIT EXERCISES

The following exercises will improve your ability to negotiate well.

Shoot for a win-win solution.

You can establish a positive tone for your negotiations by explicitly communicating up front your intention to find a win-win solution. Practice this exercise: *After realizing that a discussion has transitioned into negotiation, state that you want to find a win-win solution and ask about the other party's main concerns by saying, "It's important to me that we find a solution we are both happy with. Help me understand—what are your main concerns?"*

Solve problems together.

People are more likely to come to agreement in negotiations when they feel they are working together to solve a problem. Practice changing negotiations into collaborative problem-solving discussions using this exercise: *After hearing someone voice an idea, incorporate the idea into the discussion as an opportunity for collaborative problem-solving by saying, "How can we can use your idea to [summarize the idea] as we solve this problem together and find our ideal solution?"* For example, you could incorporate the other party's idea to sell branded products into your negotiation about the company's marketing strategy.

Highlight the benefits of your preferred solution.

By definition, win-win negotiations result in benefits for both parties. Practice explaining how your preferred solution creates a win-win scenario using this exercise: *After looking at your calendar and anticipating that a particular meeting will involve negotiation, write down in one sentence your preferred solution and what benefits it brings to both parties.* For example, if forming a strategic partnership with a reseller is your preferred solution, the benefits would come from access to new customer groups who can generate additional revenues for both you and the reseller while reducing the cost of sale, as you and the reseller would be splitting those costs.

Ask for agreement on next steps.

Negotiations can't lead to the desired outcomes unless both parties understand the next steps and agree upon them. Make it a habit to seek confirmation before leaving a discussion by practicing this exercise: *After realizing that the discussion is coming to an end, state your understanding of the next steps and ask for agreement by saying, "I understand our next steps to be . . . . Do you agree?"*

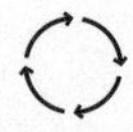

Growing People & Teams

Growing People & Teams is a category of leadership skills that focus on empowering and developing people to become better at their jobs and to grow in their personal and professional lives. As a leader, you must ensure that your followers grow their skills and stay engaged with their work, and you must retain your top performers. These leadership skills are especially important in situations when you need to increase the performance of individuals or teams; improve employee satisfaction, engagement, and retention; and build a culture of excellence. There are three leadership skills in this category: Empower Others, Mentor and Coach, and Build Team Spirit.

SKILL: Empower Others

Empowering others means giving them decision-making authority and providing support without removing responsibility. In our research, we discovered the micro-behaviors that effective leaders do when they empower others:

1. Allocate an appropriate level of decision-making authority such that others don't feel overwhelmed by responsibility at one extreme or micromanaged at the other.
2. Provide support without removing responsibility—let others own the issues they are responsible for, and provide support by acting as a consultant to them.
3. Set check-in points and corresponding milestones to monitor progress.
4. Coach others through barriers and roadblocks to help them overcome challenges.

WHY THE SKILL IS IMPORTANT FOR LEADERSHIP

To achieve better results, you need A-players on your team, and your job as a leader is to help your people develop into A-players. People grow when they are empowered to do so—when they own their decisions, feel personally responsible for outcomes, and directly experience the consequences of their actions. But if you don't empower others to make decisions, then you run the risk of creating a team of helpless individuals who simply do what you tell them but don't have the confidence or ability to think and act independently—plus you will become the decision-making bottleneck of your team.

At work, empowering others will help you to boost innovation on your team, increase employee retention and engagement, and build a high-performance culture. Effective leaders improve products, services, and operations by creating space for creativity, which means giving people room to experiment with ideas and appropriate freedom to make decisions for themselves. When employees are empowered, they feel a positive connection with their team and the organization as a whole, and they achieve superior results.

TELLTALE SIGNS YOU NEED TO IMPROVE THIS SKILL

- If you have a difficult time letting other people make decisions.
- If you feel like your input is needed for others to make the "correct" decision.
- If you like to solve problems for other people.
- If you are convinced that your advice is a gift from which others can learn.
- If you think that providing support is telling people what to do.

PERSONALITY TRAITS ALIGNED WITH THIS SKILL

If you score *high on Caring and low on Organized,* you may find empowering others intrinsically rewarding. If you are high on Caring, you are probably perceptive, supportive, and empathetic; you enjoy standing up for employees and listening to their ideas. If you are low on Organized, you are likely flexible and more tolerant of ambiguity. (In contrast, if you are high on Organized, you may be micromanaging others because of rigid, controlling, and perfectionistic tendencies.) With the combination of high on Caring and low on Organized, you are likely to derive satisfaction from behaviors like sharing decision-making authority with others, providing support without removing responsibility, or coaching people through roadblocks and barriers.

5-MINUTE LEADER HABIT EXERCISES

The following exercises will improve your ability to empower others.

Empower others by sharing decision-making authority.

When you delegate, you only assign tasks or projects to others, but when you give people the decision-making power that goes along with those tasks and projects, you empower them. Use this exercise to get in the habit of sharing decision-making authority: *After assigning a project or task to a team member, start a brief conversation on decision-making authority by saying, "What decisions related to this assignment are you comfortable making?"* For example, you could clarify that the person is comfortable making decisions about travel purchases under $2,000 in value.

Provide support without removing responsibility.

To truly empower others, you must allow them to come up with their own solutions to the issues they are responsible for. However, this doesn't mean you should have a "sink or swim" mentality. Instead, use this exercise to practice providing support to others without removing responsibility: *After someone expresses a concern or frustration, acknowledge it and ask how you can help by saying, "I understand that you feel concerned about . . . . How can I help?"*

Agree on the next check-in point.

Effective leaders monitor progress without micromanaging. You accomplish this by giving people the freedom to run with their projects as they see fit while establishing regular check-in points and milestones to ensure that the projects are on the right track. Practice the following exercise to make this a habit: *After discussing the details of someone's assignment, agree on the next check-in point by asking, "When should we check in on your progress and what deliverables should we expect to review at that point?"* For example, you could agree to check in after two weeks and review the first draft of the presentation slides.

Coach through roadblocks.

Coaching people through roadblocks doesn't mean giving advice or solving their problems for them; it means helping them to find their own solutions to the challenges they face. Use this exercise to practice asking questions instead of telling people how to solve their problems: *After someone comes to you with a problem or issue, ask questions instead of offering solutions and advice by saying, "What makes this a problem and what have you already tried?"*

SKILL: Mentor and Coach

Mentoring and coaching means actively developing others through feedback, challenging assignments, reflection, and suggestions. In our research, we discovered the micro-behaviors that effective leaders do when they mentor and coach:

1. Provide timely, behavior-focused feedback that addresses actions as opposed to characteristics (e.g., "you haven't been completing reports on time" vs. "you are lazy with your reports").
2. Support people's development with specific, useful suggestions for how to improve (e.g., brainstorm alternatives to a problem behavior).
3. Collaborate with people on drafting their development plans rather than dictating what they need to improve and how they need to do it.
4. Facilitate reflection to help people cognitively process their experiences and enhance their learning.

WHY THE SKILL IS IMPORTANT FOR LEADERSHIP

People don't develop skills by taking a class or reading a book. It's your job as their leader to actively help them develop them through feedback, challenging assignments, suggestions, and reflection. If you don't invest your time and energy into developing the people on your team, they will stop learning, stagnate, and become disengaged, and their performance will eventually decline.

At work, mentoring and coaching will help you to improve customer service, improve the performance and engagement of your team members, and build a culture of continuous improvement. Don't allow yourself to become so focused on getting things done that you overlook the importance of helping your people grow, and don't focus your coaching and mentoring efforts only on the lowest performers at the expense of everyone else. By using feedback, suggestions, and reflections to help all your employees develop their skills, you will prepare your entire team to be ready to tackle whatever challenges arise.

TELLTALE SIGNS YOU NEED TO IMPROVE THIS SKILL

- If you don't see employee development as part of your job.
- If your development recommendation is "read a book or take a class."
- If you struggle to balance getting things done with helping people to grow.
- If you focus only on coaching low performers.
- If you think that coaching is telling people how to do their jobs better.

PERSONALITY TRAITS ALIGNED WITH THIS SKILL

If you score *high on Caring,* you may find mentoring and coaching intrinsically rewarding. If you are high on Caring, you are probably perceptive and empathetic; you enjoy supporting people. With this trait, you are likely to derive satisfaction from behaviors like providing feedback, useful developmental suggestions, and facilitating reflection.

5-MINUTE LEADER HABIT EXERCISES

The following exercises will improve your ability to mentor and coach.

Provide immediate feedback.

Timely, behavior-focused feedback is the best way to help people understand what they are doing well and where they need to improve. Get in the habit of providing feedback immediately using this exercise: *After noticing a mistake in someone's work or an incorrect behavior, high-w light it right away by saying, "When [situation], you did [action], which resulted in [outcome]."* For example, "When you filled out your timesheet, you missed the second page, which will delay our ability to pay you on time."

Offer specific developmental suggestions.

This micro-behavior involves brainstorming specific behaviors a person can try to improve a skill or correct a problem behavior, other than reading books or taking classes: *After discussing an area of improvement with someone, turn the focus of the discussion to identifying a specific development suggestion by saying, "Why don't we try an experiment—what is a new and different approach you could try?"* For example, you could offer some exercises from this book as new development ideas.

Collaborate on development.

Effective coaching and mentoring is a collaboration, a dialogue between two equals who jointly work together to help one person grow. Use this exercise to make a habit of turning ordinary meetings into collaborative development dialogues and learning opportunities: *After finishing with the initial small talk during a meeting, ask what the person wants to learn today by saying, "What is your learning goal for the day?"* For example, someone may want to learn how to use a particular formula in Excel today.

Facilitate reflection.

People learn by experimenting and then reflecting on their experience to discover what worked well and what needs changing. Use this exercise to practice helping others reflect on and learn from their experiences: *After someone describes a recent experience, help them reflect on it by saying, "Why do you think it happened this way? What did you learn from it?"*

SKILL: Build Team Spirit

Building team spirit means creating a sense of cohesion on your team by linking its mission to organizational strategy and helping it accomplish its goals. In our research, we discovered the micro-behaviors that effective leaders do when they build team spirit:

1. Advocate for team cohesion—explicitly state the importance of team cohesion and its benefits for the team.
2. Establish daily team-building activities to strengthen cohesion—find everyday activities that help build relationships among teammates and make them feel more connected to the team.
3. Suggest procedures and policies to accomplish team goals—clarify the team goals and suggest how to achieve them more efficiently.
4. Link individual assignments to the team's mission—explain how individual assignments fit into the larger goals of the team and organization.

WHY THE SKILL IS IMPORTANT FOR LEADERSHIP

In any organization, people are interdependent—each person's work influences the work of many others. If individual team members don't coordinate their efforts, overall productivity suffers. As a leader, you must ensure that your team is operating as a cohesive unit.

At work, creating team cohesion is an important part of building a culture of continuous improvement, increasing employee performance and retention, and combining or restructuring business units. Continuous improvement is partly dependent on the better coordination of individual efforts that results from greater team cohesion. Cohesive teams are more productive and deliver higher-quality work because they develop stronger norms around performance standards, and all team members are expected to adhere to those standards. Similarly, people feel a stronger emotional connection to cohesive teams, which makes them more likely to stay.

TELLTALE SIGNS YOU NEED TO IMPROVE THIS SKILL

- If you only focus on managing individuals and their projects.
- If you hold fewer than two team meetings in a month.

- If you don't set team goals.
- If you don't understand how one person's work relates to someone else's.
- If you don't see your direct reports as a team.

PERSONALITY TRAITS ALIGNED WITH THIS SKILL

If you score *high on Caring*, you may find building team spirit intrinsically rewarding. If you are high on Caring, you are probably perceptive, supportive, empathetic, and cooperative; you enjoy participating in teamwork. Because of your considerate, supportive nature, you are likely to derive satisfaction from behaviors like advocating for team cohesion, establishing team-building activities, making procedural suggestions, and linking the team's mission to the bigger organizational strategy.

5-MINUTE LEADER HABIT EXERCISES

The following exercises will improve your ability to build team spirit.

Advocate for cohesion.

Teams are more effective when the individual members coordinate their efforts and share a common sense of purpose or unity. Practice explicitly discussing the importance of the team acting as one and how that benefits the team using this exercise: *After reviewing the agenda or discussion points for a team meeting, emphasize the importance of team cohesion by saying, "It is very important that we act as one; it will help us better achieve our shared goals."*

Establish daily team-building activities.

Most people think of team-building activities as being things you do off-site and after hours, such as meeting for happy hour or going bowling, but you can also facilitate stronger cohesion by creating connections between team members and others in the organization on a daily basis: *After greeting someone (in an email or in person), connect them with another person that could help them or whom they would just enjoy meeting by saying, "I think you would really enjoy meeting . . . because . . . ."* For example, you could connect people who have worked on similar projects or share similar hobbies.

Discuss a procedural improvement.

Remember that people's work is always interdependent and there are always opportunities for people to better coordinate their efforts. Practice this exercise to get in the habit of discussing procedural improvements that will help your team members better coordinate their efforts and increase the team's efficiency: *After discussing a task with someone, find a small procedural improvement by asking, "Who do you depend on to get your work done, and how can you better coordinate efforts with this person?"* For example, a colleague in accounting provides you with monthly statements of product usage, but you need updates on a weekly basis to better manage your accounts.

Link individual assignments with your team's purpose.

Practice helping people to connect the dots between their own work and the goals of the team and organization using this exercise: *After reviewing what someone is working on, highlight how that project or task supports the team's mission by saying, "Your work on . . . is very important for our team's mission to . . . ."* For example, "Your work on the social media campaign is very important for our team's mission to reduce smoking in young adults."

Interpersonal Skills

Interpersonal Skills is a category of leadership skills that focus on building relationships and communicating with people. As a leader, you work with people on a daily basis, so you need to quickly develop strong working relationships. You also need to be able to listen to people's concerns and communicate clearly so that everyone understands what to do. These leadership skills are important to accomplishing almost any goal in any situation. There are five leadership skills in this category: Build Strategic Relationships, Show Caring, Listen Actively, Communicate Clearly, and Speak with Charisma.

SKILL: Build Strategic Relationships

Building strategic relationships means quickly establishing rapport with key people and proactively strengthening those relationships. In our research, we discovered the micro-behaviors that effective leaders do when they build relationships:

1. Identify which relationships should be initiated or improved and prioritize which relationships are more and less critical to develop first.
2. Offer and provide support to key people (e.g., volunteer additional assistance and suggestions).
3. Capitalize on common interests and areas of agreement to build rapport (e.g., highlight similar goals).
4. Create win-win opportunities for both parties.

WHY THE SKILL IS IMPORTANT FOR LEADERSHIP

The nature of your work relationships will determine your ability to get things done. If you have poor relationships with your followers or others in your organization, it may result in conflicts and low trust, and ultimately undermine performance. On the one hand, if you are too direct or tough on people, it will be difficult for you to motivate them and keep them engaged with their work and the organization. They may get offended and begin to resent you and their work. On the other hand, if you are withdrawn, soft-spoken, and generally awkward in social settings, you will struggle to build rapport with people. Either way, it is difficult to be an effective leader without building strong relationships.

At work, relationship-building skills also enable you to create strategic alliances with suppliers, vendors, and other partners outside your organization. Establishing mutually beneficial relationships with other firms is critical to successfully pursuing common business goals.

TELLTALE SIGNS YOU NEED TO IMPROVE THIS SKILL

- If you are shy, soft-spoken, and withdrawn.
- If you feel awkward in social settings.
- If you just care about getting the work done and relationships with people are unimportant to you.
- If you pride yourself on being direct with people and telling it like it is.
- If you get impatient with small talk and just want to dive straight into the agenda.

PERSONALITY TRAITS ALIGNED WITH THIS SKILL

If you score *high on Outgoing and high on Caring,* you may find building relationships intrinsically rewarding. If you are high on Outgoing, relationship-building behaviors may come to you naturally. Your charming style probably makes you a good conversationalist, and you are likely able to quickly build rapport with others. You are probably friendly and have an open and honest style, which further contributes to your ability to build strong relationships with people. If you are high on Caring, you are probably perceptive, supportive, empathetic, and cooperative. You may be considerate and show regard for employees as people, show appreciation for their work, and stand up for employees. With this combination of traits, you are likely to derive satisfaction from building strategic relationships.

5-MINUTE LEADER HABIT EXERCISES

The following exercises will improve your ability to build relationships.

Initiate relationships.

Effective leaders don't wait for other people to seek them out; they initiate and build relationships proactively. Use this exercise to practice initiating contact and developing relationships: *After sitting down at your desk to start your workday, write down the name of one person with whom you need to initiate contact or strengthen your relationship and reach out with an email or a phone call.*

Offer and provide support.

Helping others is an effective way to create and strengthen relationships. Practice this exercise to make it a habit: *After hearing someone voice a request, immediately offer to help by saying, "I'd be happy to assist you with that. What would be most helpful for you?"* For example, you could send a relevant article or make an introduction to an expert in that area.

Find common interests.

Rapport comes from similar goals and interests. To build rapport with others, find out what you have in common; there are probably more things than you realize. Use this exercise to practice identifying common interests, values, hobbies, opinions, and experiences with other people: *After meeting with someone, write down two things that you have in common. Refer back to one of these similarities in your next email or in-person interaction.* For example, you could both enjoy football or come from the same state.

Create win-win opportunities.

Win-win opportunities strengthen relationships. Practice highlighting how a proposed solution will benefit both parties using this exercise: *After discussing an action item, state one benefit each party would enjoy by saying,*

"I see this as a win-win solution for both of us. You will benefit by . . . and I will benefit by . . . ." For example, an expatriate assignment would provide valuable international experience for your trusted employee, and you would be confident knowing you have a skilled person whom you can count on leading operations in that region.

SKILL: Show Caring

Showing caring means demonstrating genuine concern for others' well-being. In our research, we discovered the micro-behaviors that effective leaders do when they show caring:

1. Communicate with others in a polite and respectful manner—never rude, arrogant, or aggressive.
2. Explicitly use words and phrases that communicate caring, e.g., "Your satisfaction matters a great deal to me."
3. Use language that expresses your appreciation of others and values their contributions, e.g., "I value your input on this issue."
4. Directly address the emotion a person is feeling by naming the emotion and acknowledging that you see it, either in discussion or in writing.

WHY THE SKILL IS IMPORTANT FOR LEADERSHIP

Showing that you care about other people goes a long way toward building trust and strong relationships with them. If your followers know that you care about them, they will reciprocate and care about you. This creates a culture of mutual respect, loyalty, and dedication, and inspires people to put in extra effort to achieve ambitious goals and meet important deadlines.

At work, showing people that you care for them will enable you to increase employee satisfaction, engagement, and retention. Caring is at the heart of the positive connection employees feel toward the company, and it increases their desire to work hard and remain.

TELLTALE SIGNS YOU NEED TO IMPROVE THIS SKILL

- If you see work life and personal life as completely separate spheres and you know nothing about your followers' personal lives.
- If you are too busy with your work to care about someone's personal problems.
- If you can't read emotions and don't know when someone is happy or frustrated.
- If someone described you as rude and arrogant in the past.
- If you take a long time to warm up to people.

PERSONALITY TRAITS ALIGNED WITH THIS SKILL

If you score *high on Caring*, you may find showing caring intrinsically rewarding. If you are high on Caring, you are probably perceptive and empathetic; you enjoy supporting people. With this trait, you are likely to derive satisfaction from behaviors like communicating in a polite and respectful manner, making others feel valued and appreciated, and letting people know that you understand their emotions.

5-MINUTE LEADER HABIT EXERCISES

The following exercises will improve your ability to show caring.

Be polite and respectful.

You are probably polite and respectful most of the time, except when you are stressed or irritated. Practice this exercise to make a habit of remaining polite and respectful even under pressure: *After noticing even the slightest frustration or irritation, say, "Thank you for bringing this to my attention. Let me have a think and come back to you later."*

Use caring phrases.

The language we use is a reflection of our attitudes and beliefs, and vice versa. The more caring language you use, the more attuned you will be to the well-being of others. Practice saying at least one caring phrase a day using this exercise: *After hearing someone voice a concern, say a caring phrase, such as, "It's important to me that we resolve your concerns. I want to make sure that your needs are met."*

Make others feel valued and appreciated.

We all want to feel valued and appreciated for who we are and what we contribute. Practice telling at least one person a day either in an email or in person that you value and appreciate something about them using this exercise: *After realizing that the discussion or email is coming to an end, say, "I want you to know that I value/appreciate . . . ."* For example, you could say that you value the person's input on the issue, or appreciate their hard work.

Name that emotion.

Acknowledging and naming emotions is a powerful way to let others know that you are attentive to them and that you care about their well-being. Use this exercise to practice directly addressing the emotion a person is feeling: *After someone expresses an emotion, either in person or in an email, have a quick discussion or send a reply to understand why they're feeling that way by saying, "You seemed [emotion], and I wonder if you'd like to talk about it."* For example, your colleague could be happy because his child passed a tough math exam, or he could be sad because his father is seriously ill.

SKILL: Listen Actively

Listening actively means hearing and comprehending another by asking insightful questions and checking your own understanding. In our research, we discovered the micro-behaviors that effective leaders do when they listen actively:

1. Ask open-ended rather than close-ended questions. Start open-ended questions with *what*, *how*, or *why*.
2. Restate, summarize, and clarify what you hear during conversations.
3. Ask probing questions to achieve deeper insight and identify the root cause of problems.

WHY THE SKILL IS IMPORTANT FOR LEADERSHIP

Listening is a core leadership skill. You can't understand the problems on your team and accurately resolve them if you don't listen to what people have to say. No matter your intellect, you don't have all the answers. To be an effective leader, you need to consult with others and learn from them—and you can only do that with strong listening skills. If you cut people off, finish their sentences, or think about what you'll say next while someone is speaking, you are not listening to them and so you won't get the answers you need to solve important team and organizational problems.

At work, actively listening will help you to increase employee satisfaction, engagement, and performance. If you listen to people, you communicate to them that you care about their input and ideas and you take them into consideration when making decisions. Not only does this additional input enhance the quality of your decision, but by actively listening to your employees, you make them feel more appreciated and engaged.

TELLTALE SIGNS YOU NEED TO IMPROVE THIS SKILL

- If you don't remember what was discussed in a meeting.
- If you frequently ask people to repeat what they said because you missed the point.
- If you interrupt people or finish their sentences.
- If you think about what you'll say next when someone else is speaking.
- If you spend most of the time talking.

PERSONALITY TRAITS ALIGNED WITH THIS SKILL

If you score *low on Outgoing and high on Caring,* you may find listening intrinsically rewarding. If you are low on Outgoing, you are probably composed and reserved; you enjoy listening. (In contrast, if you are very high on Outgoing, you are probably overly talkative and don't listen to others.) If you are high on Caring, you are probably perceptive and empathetic; you enjoy getting along with people and getting to know them. With the combination of low on Outgoing and high on Caring, you are likely to derive satisfaction from behaviors like asking open-ended questions, restating and summarizing what the other person said, and asking questions to stimulate deeper insight.

5-MINUTE LEADER HABIT EXERCISES

The following exercises will improve your ability to listen actively.

Ask open-ended questions.

Open-ended questions encourage people to talk more and create opportunities for genuine conversation because they require more than a simple yes-or-no answer. Use this exercise to make a habit of starting your questions with "what" or "how": *After realizing that you want to ask a question, start it with the words "what" or "how."* For example, you could ask, "What is your position on this? What else matters to you? How is this different from your expectations?"

Restate and summarize.

Restating and summarizing what other people say to you lets them know that you are listening and provides an opportunity to check your understanding of what you heard. Use this exercise to make it a habit: *After someone explains an idea or experience they've had, restate and summarize what they said by saying, "What I heard you say is . . . ."*

Ask probing questions.

Good probing questions, especially when they explore people's assumptions, stimulate deeper processing of information, promote critical thinking, and can help identify the root causes of problems. Use this exercise to make a habit of asking about people's underlying assumptions: *After hearing someone complain about something, ask, "What assumptions are you making when you say . . . ?"* For example, you may complain that someone cut your meeting short because you are assuming that the person is a jerk, but it could be that he is responding to a work emergency.

SKILL: Communicate Clearly

Communicating clearly means composing a focused, well-organized message that consists of a few key points. In our research, we discovered the micro-behaviors that effective leaders do when they communicate clearly:

1. Include only relevant thoughts and information in the message; omit irrelevant or unnecessary information.
2. Use a clear structure and organize the message around a few key points.

3. Respond with a short and pointed message, rather than overwhelming the audience with data.

WHY THE SKILL IS IMPORTANT FOR LEADERSHIP

Communicating clearly is a core leadership skill. Your followers look to you for direction and priorities. If they can't understand what you are trying to communicate to them, they won't know what to do, and your team's performance will suffer as a result. Every other leadership skill described in this book becomes more effective when paired with clear communication.

At work, communicating clearly is important to achieving most business goals. One area where this skill is especially valuable is in trying to differentiate your products and services from the competition. Distinguishing products and services from competing offerings is one of the most difficult tasks that modern business leaders face, because most markets are saturated and customers have many options to choose from. Your customers can only understand why your product is better if you clearly communicate those differences in a short, pointed, easy-to-remember message.

TELLTALE SIGNS YOU NEED TO IMPROVE THIS SKILL

- If you are uncomfortable with public speaking.
- If you are a "fly by the seat of your pants" type of person.
- If you prepare your presentations at the very last minute and don't rehearse them.
- If you don't give your audience two or three key takeaways.
- If people comment on how much you like to talk.

PERSONALITY TRAITS ALIGNED WITH THIS SKILL

If you score *high on Ambitious, high on Outgoing, and high on Organized,* you may find communicating clearly intrinsically rewarding. If you are high on Ambitious, you are probably confident and energetic. If you are high on Outgoing, you are probably charming, talkative, dynamic, and enthusiastic; you enjoy interacting with other people. If you are high on Organized, you are probably methodical, systematic, and diligent; you enjoy organizing your ideas. With this combination of traits, you are likely to derive satisfaction from behaviors like including only relevant thoughts in your messages and organizing the message around key points.

5-MINUTE LEADER HABIT EXERCISES

The following exercises will improve your ability to communicate clearly.

Include only relevant thoughts and information.

Keep your messages focused by including only relevant thoughts and information. Use this exercise to make a habit of cutting unnecessary words: *After you finish writing an email, reread it and cut out as many unnecessary words as you can. Can you even delete an entire sentence?*

Organize the message around key points.

The structure of your message is as important as the words you choose. A message organized around a few key points is more effective than one that delivers the same information without a clear structure. Use this exercise to make a habit of creating an outline before you start writing a new document (an email, memo, presentation, etc.): *After opening a new word-processing document, create a quick outline of the three main points that you want your reader/audience to take away from your message.*

Respond with a short and pointed message.

It is easy to overwhelm people with complicated messages and too much information. Even when dealing with complex issues, it is usually best to keep individual messages focused on a single, clear goal. Use this exercise to practice having only one clear goal in mind when responding to other people: *After you finish reading an email, ask yourself, "What is my ultimate goal? What do I want the person to do differently?" Write it down, then compose your reply based on that one goal.* For example, your ultimate goal could be to appease the concerned customer, and so you would want the customer to feel comforted by your response.

SKILL: Speak with Charisma

Speaking with charisma means communicating with energy and passion, often using stories, similes, and metaphors to make your message more powerful and memorable. In our research, we discovered the micro-behaviors that effective leaders do when they speak with charisma:

1. Communicate with energy, excitement, and passion throughout the message or presentation.
2. Ask people to imagine a different future and use vivid, engaging, and high-impact words like assert, emerge, enhance, escalate, manifest, proclaim, strengthen, unveil, and so on.
3. Use stories, similes, and metaphors to convey ideas.

WHY THE SKILL IS IMPORTANT FOR LEADERSHIP

Passion and energy are contagious. Speaking with charisma will help you to inspire and excite your followers and call them to action. But if your speaking style is flat and unengaging, people will stop paying attention, and they won't remember what you said. Perhaps you are shy or get nervous when presenting to a large audience. Perhaps you are not passionate about the topic or you don't care about the company's vision. Or perhaps you often feel stressed, exhausted, and overwhelmed, and you come across to others as having no energy.

At work, speaking with charisma will help you to connect with your team members, keep them focused and engaged, and inspire them to complete projects on time. If you appear disengaged and unenthusiastic, you cannot expect anyone else to be excited about the team's work and the company's direction.

TELLTALE SIGNS YOU NEED TO IMPROVE THIS SKILL

- If you have a flat affect or are not a dynamic individual.
- If you are shy and get nervous when speaking to other people.
- If you have a hard time showing your passion.
- If you are often tired and lack energy during interactions.

PERSONALITY TRAITS ALIGNED WITH THIS SKILL

If you score *high on Ambitious and high on Outgoing*, you may find speaking with charisma intrinsically rewarding. If you are high on Ambitious, you are probably confident and energetic. If you are high on Outgoing, you are probably charming, talkative, dynamic, and enthusiastic; you enjoy interacting with other people. With this combination of traits, you are likely to derive satisfaction from behaviors like communicating with passion and energy, using vivid and impactful words, and using stories and similes to convey ideas.

5-MINUTE LEADER HABIT EXERCISES

The following exercises will improve your ability to speak with charisma.

Show your excitement.

We naturally respond with interest when other people are passionate, energetic, or excited. Getting in the habit of showing your excitement on a daily basis will help you to be more charismatic and engaging. Use this exercise to practice: *After greeting someone, start the small talk with a story, quote, information, or statistic you feel passionate about by saying, "I found this very interesting story . . . ."* For example, you could say that you found out that 65 percent of iPhone users say that they cannot live without their device.

Ask people to imagine.

To create a vivid experience for other people, practice asking them to imagine a different future using this exercise: *After discussing an issue, ask the person to imagine a different outcome by saying, "Imagine how different things would be if . . . ."* For example, you ask the person to imagine how different things would be if their problem suddenly went away.

Use similes and metaphors.

Similes and metaphors make descriptions more vivid and engaging for your audience. You can practice thinking of similes to convey your ideas using this exercise: *After stating your idea, quickly think about what it reminds you of by saying, "It is like . . ."* For example, you might describe a new smartphone app for dental hygiene as being "like a Fitbit that helps you track how often you brush and floss your teeth."

PART IV

ENCOURAGE NEW SKILLS IN OTHERS

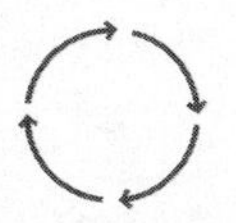

CHAPTER 8

Motivating Change

In the first three parts of this book, you learned how the Leader Habit Formula works and how to use it to become a better leader. Part IV is meant for those who want to help other people develop leadership skills. Whether you are a parent, a teacher, an athletic coach, a corporate manager, a Human Resources or Organizational Development professional, a leadership consultant, an executive coach or life coach, or someone in any number of other mentoring roles, the following chapters provide guidance for implementing the Formula in a variety of leadership development scenarios, from one-on-one and team contexts to formal programs. But before you learn how to use the Formula as a coaching and mentoring tool, you need to understand where people find the motivation to change their behavior in the first place.

Habits Start and End with Motivation

As a mentor or coach, you understand that it takes hard work and perseverance for people to learn new skills and behaviors. You also know that, as with any change, the difference between success and failure when it comes to personal development is often a matter of motivation. If people aren't genuinely motivated to change, then they won't be motivated to put in the effort necessary to make the change happen. This is as true of learning leadership skills as it is of eliminating bad habits like drinking too much alcohol. So it should come as no surprise that the Leader Habit Formula is only effective if people are motivated to practice the daily exercises until they become habits.

But here's the problem: Most people enter leadership development with baggage from previous self-help or professional development sessions. They have been through countless hours of classroom training, they have tried every new management fad, and they have been disappointed by the results. It's hard for people to be motivated for yet more training when they're not convinced it will make a difference in their lives. It's also hard for people to admit that they need to improve their skills. Many of us are like Laura the ER nurse, unaware of our weaknesses and certain that we're already effective leaders.

Your challenge as a mentor or coach is to help people find the motivation to change, and to build new habits and develop new skills through focused, consistent practice. As you probably know, this is easier said than done—human beings can be incredibly resistant to change—but it *is* possible. Once people are motivated, they can accomplish almost anything.

The Story of Ruth

Perhaps the most impressive of all habit changes is when a person overcomes an addiction. William R. Miller, who dedicated his career to studying bad habits and behavior change, described addiction as fundamentally a motivational problem—an addict persists in his or her addiction behavior despite many negative consequences, defying common sense.[1]

To show just how this works, I'll share Ruth's story. She was thirty-one when she woke up one Monday morning in the hospital, recovering from an accidental overdose. She had spent Sunday drinking wine alone and self-medicating with anti-anxiety pills. The alcohol and pills had been an attempt to calm her nerves. The night before, Saturday, Ruth had been drunk at a networking event when she made a gruesome joke in front of her clients and coworkers. It was a dirty joke so explicit that everyone in the group immediately turned bright red. Everyone felt so uncomfortable that, if they could, they would have all just pretended that those words had never left Ruth's mouth. But Ruth said those words and there was no denying that Ruth was drunk at a work function.

After the incident, her colleagues and clients had spent the rest of the night avoiding Ruth, and within hours she was feeling miserable about what she had said. It wasn't the first time alcohol had caused regrets—in fact, drunken, unfiltered, and inappropriate comments with friends and family members had become something of a regular occurrence for her over the years—but this time was worse than usual because it happened at a business function. By Sunday morning, Ruth found herself consumed by feelings of self-loathing, shame, and guilt. Still hung over, she decided a glass of wine and a pill would make her feel better. They didn't. The more she thought about what had happened, the more unpleasant memories of other alcohol-fueled mistakes came to mind, and the worse she felt. So she kept drinking and taking pills. This went on throughout the day, until she blacked out and ended up in the emergency room.

It probably won't surprise you to learn that Ruth is an alcoholic. What might surprise you, however, is the fact that Ruth didn't see herself as an alcoholic until she woke up in the hospital after her overdose.

It wasn't that Ruth had never considered the possibility she was an alcoholic. In fact, she had first wondered if she might have a problem with alcohol years earlier, when she was twenty-six and woke up in a stranger's house with no memory of where she was or how she got there. Shaken by the feeling that she was out of control, she went to a meeting of Alcoholics Anonymous that day and decided to quit drinking. After three months without so much as a drop of alcohol, she thought, "If I can go this long, I'm not an alcoholic." She bought herself a nice bottle of wine to celebrate, drank it alone that night, and slipped right back into her bad habits without realizing she was in denial.

This became Ruth's pattern of behavior: She would drink heavily for a while, then give up alcohol completely for a few months to reassure herself that she didn't have a problem, then start drinking again. She repeated the pattern for years, firmly in denial until the shock of her overdose forced her to confront the reality of her situation. The overdose was Ruth's "rock bottom"; after waking up in the hospital, she could no longer deny her addiction or rationalize her self-destructive behavior. She finally admitted to herself that she was an alcoholic, and the only way she could fix her life was to change her habit and stop drinking for good.

A few days after her overdose, Ruth started therapy, rejoined Alcoholics Anonymous, and hired a personal trainer; she hasn't had a drink since. Today she is an award-winning interior designer. Her work has been featured in prominent home magazines, and she runs her own firm designing residential and commercial spaces around the United States, including New York, San Francisco, Chicago, Seattle, and Denver. Changing her life wasn't easy, but she succeeded because of the motivation she found when she hit rock bottom.

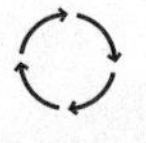

Self-Image, Internal Tension, and Transformative Insights

Hitting rock bottom is often described by those who experience it as a "wake-up call" that causes them to make difficult changes in their lives. For alcoholics and drug addicts, researchers have found that hitting rock bottom is one of the top predictors of whether a person will seek and complete treatment to get sober.[2] The motivation that comes from the experience is powerful, as Ruth and many others can attest. It is also widely misunderstood.

According to popular belief, hitting rock bottom helps people to recognize the negative consequences of their behavior, and it is their desire to avoid these negative consequences in the future that motivates them to change. In Ruth's case, the assumption would be that it was the fear of death that caused her to give up drinking. This interpretation is wrong, however. Ruth's overdose motivated her to get sober not because it made her understand that her drinking was damaging her relationships and putting her life at risk, but because it caused her to reevaluate her self-image and realize that her behavior was not consistent with who she thought she was. Until waking up in the hospital, she saw herself as a successful, ambitious, young professional woman who made smart decisions and was in control of her life. Through the power of denial, she had always been able to convince herself that her habit of regularly drinking too much didn't contradict her self-image. But drinking alone and self-medicating with pills until she had to be rushed to the emergency room? That was *not* how she pictured her life. For the first time, she was able to see past her denial and admit to herself that she was an alcoholic. Only then was she motivated to seek therapy and change her behavior.

Hitting rock bottom is an emotional, often negative, and highly subjective experience—what constitutes hitting bottom for one person won't be the same for someone else. Despite this subjectivity, all such experiences share two things in common: They force a reevaluation of a person's *self-image*, and they produce a *transformational insight* that results from the realization that the person's behavior is in conflict with his or her self-image.

To understand how transformational insights come about, researchers at the University of Memphis studied people who had made dramatic changes in their lives. The researchers found that transformational insights are usually produced in response to experiences that people interpret as painful or uncertain. For example, one participant in the study decided to abandon the culture of her home country and redefined her self-image after an upsetting visit to her homeland. Another participant realized that he needed to learn to rely on himself after experiencing poverty and not being able to find food for three days.[3]

For the people in this study, as for Ruth, the transformative insight came when an unexpected situation made them question their self-image and realize that the assumptions they held about themselves were incorrect. The experience was so distressing that it shook their internal beliefs about who they were as people. They couldn't easily ignore or dismiss what had happened—there was no more room for denial—and they couldn't rationalize the experience or explain it away. The only choice was to do something about it.

Confronting a negative reality, as Ruth did, creates internal tension. The internal tension Ruth experienced forced her to think honestly about her past behaviors, contrast those behaviors with how she pictured her life (her self-image), and explore what the conflict between the reality of her behavior and her self-image meant for her most deeply held beliefs. Working through the strong emotions and confusion caused by this conflict ultimately led Ruth to a better understanding of herself and triggered her transformational insight (*I'm an alcoholic; I need to change my life and get sober*). This new knowledge created the motivation Ruth needed to give up alcohol and change her habits so that her behavior would be consistent with her self-image.

When coaching or mentoring others, you can only be successful if the people you are working with are motivated to change. You might be tempted to try to motivate them with negative consequences, like the threat of losing a job. Resist this temptation. It is counterproductive and will only create resistance, as I will discuss later in this chapter. Instead, focus on helping people achieve transformative insights, which create a genuine motivation to change.

The Unskilled Are Clueless

Transformative insights rarely come easily, but for some people they are more difficult to achieve than you might expect. Let's do a quick experiment: Compared to other drivers in your state, are you better than average? The same as average? Or worse than average?

If you're like most people, you believe you are a better-than-average driver. In fact, when researchers at the University of Oregon posed the same question in a survey, *93 percent of people rated their driving ability as better than average.*[4] This finding defies mathematical possibility—93 percent of people cannot, by definition, be better-than-average drivers. Average in this admittedly oversimplified context means the middle point of a distribution of all drivers, so one-half of drivers would be worse than average and the other half would be better. But that is not how people view themselves. No matter the activity, people always think that they are better than average.

This should come as no surprise. As you will recall from Chapter 5, people are generally bad at self-assessment; they have a tendency to grossly overestimate their ability and inflate their self-image. What might surprise you, however, is that the effect is most pronounced for the *lowest performers*. People who are the worst at a task have the most unrealistic self-image—they think they are much better than they actually are.

A simple experiment with college students demonstrated this effect. Right after finishing an in-class exam and before seeing their results, researchers asked the students to estimate how many questions they answered correctly. As would be expected based on people's tendency to overestimate their ability, on average, the students thought that they knew the course material 22 percent better than their performance on the test indicated. Then the researchers split the students into quartiles based on their actual scores on the exam. When the researchers studied the estimates of the bottom quartile of students (the worst performers), they found something truly worrying: The lowest performers overestimated their own abilities dramatically more than any other group. On average, students receiving the lowest scores on the exam thought they knew the course content better than they actually did by a staggering 48 percent—more than double the overestimation of all students combined.[5]

Why is it that the worst performers are the ones who think they are much better than they actually are, more so than everybody else? For one, people who don't have a skill also lack the ability to accurately assess how far they are from mastery—they don't know what they don't know. When people are first learning a skill, they make mistakes. This is natural, and with proper feedback, the knowledge that we are making mistakes is what helps us to improve our performance. But those who completely lack the skill don't benefit from this learning cycle because *they can't even recognize when they are making mistakes*. If you don't know that you are making mistakes, it is only natural that you will tend to overestimate your abilities even more than you would otherwise.

Ignorance becomes a double curse for the unskilled. They make many mistakes because they don't have the skills they need, and their lack of skill makes it impossible to recognize when they make mistakes. Unaware of their deficiencies and their mistakes, they don't know that they need to improve their skills, so they go through life clueless, thinking that they are much better performers than they actually are.

Remember how Laura the ER nurse was surprised that she was not being promoted into management? Or how John didn't know that others saw him as authoritarian and indifferent to their concerns? Both individuals lacked critical leadership skills, yet they thought that they were ready to step into more prominent leadership roles because they both didn't know what they didn't know. Laura didn't know that she was a poor listener whom her colleagues saw as argumentative, sarcastic, and difficult to work with. Because she lacked active listening skills, she didn't know what it meant to be a good listener, and she didn't know how far her behavior was from that ideal. Similarly, John couldn't tell that people resented his leadership style and were disengaged from their work. Unaware of his mistakes, he interpreted others' compliance as commitment.

The unskilled are, indeed, clueless. They don't know what they don't know, and they don't even realize when they make mistakes. In order to improve their skills, they must first experience a transformational insight that helps them to realize their lack of skill and motivates them to put in the effort necessary to change their behavior. And yet the methods of training and instruction that underlie traditional leadership development programs rarely produce transformational insights for anyone, unskilled or otherwise. Why is that?

Because we have been taught that giving critical feedback is the best way to get people to change, when in fact nothing could be further from the truth.

Critical Feedback Won't Produce Transformative Insights

In Aesop's fable of *The Fox and the Grapes*, one day a thirsty fox came upon a bunch of grapes hanging from a vine. The grapes were just the thing the fox needed to satisfy his thirst, but they were high above the ground. The fox jumped for the grapes and missed. He tried again, this time with a running start, but still the grapes were too high. Upset that he couldn't reach them, the fox turned his nose up at the grapes and thought, "They must be sour anyway."

Aesop's fable memorably illustrates the human proclivity for denial: like the fox, people tend to explain away their failures and shortcomings rather than admitting them. It's a universal tendency, as common today as it was in ancient Greece, especially when it comes to critical feedback.

Imagine that you visit your doctor for your annual physical exam. The nurse takes your temperature and blood pressure and gives you a set of health-related questionnaires to fill out. Then the physician comes to the room and proceeds to inform you about a newly discovered medical condition called "TAA deficiency," in which the body fails to produce an enzyme called thioamine acetylase. Although you might not have any symptoms now, your doctor explains that this condition can lead to serious health problems later in life. She offers you the option to take a simple saliva test that was developed just six months ago. You agree. So you spit a bit of saliva into a cup, dip a strip of colorless paper into the cup, and wait for the strip to turn dark green. Your doctor explained that the test paper reacts to the presence of TAA in saliva by changing color. But if your saliva doesn't contain TAA (when you have the deficiency), the test paper will stay unchanged. You wait a few seconds and take a look. The paper hasn't changed color. You give it a few more seconds. Still nothing. Questions start to race through your mind. Is it really possible that you have TAA deficiency? How serious is the condition anyway? Is the saliva test even accurate?

As you have probably guessed, TAA deficiency isn't a real medical condition. It was made up by researchers at Kent State University as part of a clever psychological experiment to test how people respond to negative feedback. Using a similar scenario to the one I described above, some college students were told they had TAA deficiency after the test paper (which was just a regular strip of construction paper) failed to turn green upon contact with their saliva; other students were told that an unchanged test paper meant that they were healthy and didn't have the condition. The researchers were interested in measuring students' reactions to the unfavorable diagnosis. They asked all participants to rate how serious they saw the disease and how accurate they believed the saliva test to be.

Just as Aesop's fox convinced himself that the grapes he couldn't reach must be sour, the students deceived into thinking they had TAA deficiency responded with denial. They viewed the condition as less serious and more common than did the "healthy" students in the control group. The deceived students also viewed the saliva test as less accurate than did the healthy students. When asked to think of recent irregularities in their lives, the students who were told they had TAA deficiency wrote down more examples than did students in the healthy group.[6] Faced with unfavorable information, the deceived students did their best to explain it away with alternative explanations for their positive test results.

Why were these students so dismissive of the test result? Why couldn't they just accept the diagnosis? Because it contradicted their self-image. Most people think of themselves as being healthy; it's part of who they are. When the students were confronted with information about their health that contradicted their self-image, it created the same kind of internal tension that Ruth experienced after her overdose, and without realizing it they immediately started looking for ways to eliminate that tension.

People describe internal tension in different ways—they might call it stress or anxiety, or say their head is spinning, or they might feel fearful or guilty or ashamed, or they might experience some other negative emotion or sensation. Regardless of how it is described, internal tension is uncomfortable because we generally like to act in ways that are consistent with our self-image. Think back to the pizza delivery drivers and homeowners you read about in Chapter 4. Once the delivery drivers began to think of themselves as safe drivers, they started not only buckling up but also using their turn signals, because both of those behaviors are what safe drivers do.[7] Similarly, once the homeowners started thinking of themselves as supporters of safe driving, they were willing to have a massive billboard installed in their front yard, because they saw it as something that advocates of safe driving would do.[8]

The important thing to remember is that people feel most comfortable when their behavior matches their definition of who they are—it's a good strategy to avoid internal tension. But when people do something that contradicts their self-image, they feel the pain of the inconsistency and do their best to escape it.

When people experience internal tension from something that is inconsistent with their self-image, there are only three things they can do to get their mind back into balance: (1) they can dismiss, ignore, or explain away the behavior as an exception; (2) they can change their behavior; or (3) they can change their self-image.

Of course, Option 1, denial, is the easiest, and we all have a lot of practice with it. The struggling dieter thinks, "I did so well yesterday that I can cheat today and have the cookie." The recovering alcoholic thinks, "I went three months without drinking, so I must not be addicted." The naïve employee thinks, "My boss doesn't like me, and that's why she is giving me this negative performance review." Options 2 and 3 are much more difficult because changing your behavior and changing your self-image both require a lot of time and effort. In contrast, denial is a quick way to resolve internal tension, and it's almost effortless. No wonder it's the most popular choice for dealing with information that contradicts how we see ourselves—especially critical feedback.

At Arizona State University, researchers asked working MBA students to rate themselves on a set of twenty-six leadership skills and also to give a similar questionnaire to their boss. After seeing the feedback from their boss, the students were surveyed on how accurate they considered that feedback. Given people's tendency to overestimate their own ability, the higher the ratings the students received from their boss, the more the students saw the feedback as accurate. Better feedback aligned more closely with the students' inflated perceptions of their own abilities, and thus to their self-image, making them more likely to accept the feedback.

But what happened when the feedback was critical and contradicted the students' self-image? To study that question, the researchers subtracted the ratings received from the students' boss from the students' self-assessed ratings. For example, if a student rated himself "5" on a skill but his boss rated him "3," the difference would be 5 – 3 = 2. The larger this "discrepancy number," the more the feedback from one's boss differed from one's self-image. After analyzing the data, the researchers found a negative correlation between the students' discrepancy number and their perceptions of the accuracy of the feedback they had received. In other words, when bosses gave students lower ratings than the students gave themselves, the students didn't believe that the feedback was accurate. Moreover, the bigger the difference between the students' self-rating and the rating from their boss, the less accurate the boss's critical feedback was perceived to be by the students.[9]

The conclusion we can draw from the Arizona State University study is simple, and probably won't come as a surprise if you've ever given or received criticism: *The further away critical feedback is from our self-image, the more likely we are to dismiss or rationalize it.*

This poses a special problem for the unskilled, the worst performers. Remember, it's the lowest performers who overestimate their skills the most and whose self-image is furthest from reality. When they receive critical feedback, the criticism seems to them completely inaccurate because it is so different from how they see themselves. In their minds, it isn't possible that they're not high performers (remember that they're ignorant of their mistakes), so they go straight to Option 1, denial: "He is biased against me . . . . He doesn't really know me . . . . He doesn't like me . . . . This is the first time I am hearing this, so it can't be true . . . . I was just having a bad day . . . ." The list of rationalizations is probably infinite, and trying to counter them is futile because you will only create more denial and more resistance. And as long as someone is in denial, the end result will always be the same: The person won't achieve a transformative insight and won't be motivated to change.

Our mistaken belief that critical feedback motivates people to change is the same as our misunderstanding of what makes hitting bottom a transformative life experience—it all stems from the incorrect notion that people change their behavior in order to avoid negative consequences. The standard approach of giving critical feedback and directly or indirectly telling people "change or else" is an attempt to create the negative consequences we assume will motivate them to change. But as you've seen, this approach is almost sure to backfire, especially for the people who most need to develop their skills and form new habits. The critical feedback that people receive is usually inconsistent with their self-image, more so for the worst performers, and people respond to the internal tension of this inconsistency by dismissing the criticism as inaccurate, no matter how objectively sound the feedback is. Frustrated by such denial, we usually resort to giving advice or coercing people into training, neither of which fosters motivation to change. Our advice gets ignored, people sit through training that does little to improve their skills, and the cycle of futility repeats. But there must be another way, something that you can do as a coach or mentor to help others gain the transformational insights they need to change.

Thankfully there is, and it starts with keeping your criticism and advice to yourself.

Keep Your Advice to Yourself

Before the 1980s, the standard approach to addiction treatment resembled how most leadership development programs are run today—change was imposed on people, treatment consisted of often coercive solutions full of expert advice, and denial and poor motivation were seen as problems on the side of the patient.

Then in the early 1980s, clinical psychologist William R. Miller looked at patient resistance in a new light, and his insights changed the course of addiction treatment. Rather than seeing resistance and low motivation as problems that were the patient's fault, Miller started to view it as problems caused by the therapist. Miller knew that therapists didn't intend to create resistance and low motivation in their patients, but he realized they were doing so nonetheless through the coercive and confrontational methods that were the accepted standard of care. To change this counterproductive dynamic, he developed a new therapeutic technique called *motivational interviewing.*[10]

Motivational interviewing is based on the principle that motivation to change must come from *within* a person; it cannot be imposed by someone else, and no one can be coerced to change. You might think this approach diminishes the role of the therapist—all she can do is bide her time and wait until the patient has a transformative insight—but that is not the case. Instead, the therapist guides her patient to the crucial insight by actively developing the internal tension between the patient's self-image and his behavior. In this way, the therapist helps the patient find the internal motivation to change.

To better understand the difference between motivational interviewing and the confrontational approach that most people are familiar with, let's return to Laura the ER nurse and imagine how my coaching discussion with her would have unfolded if I tried to use critical feedback and advice to get her to change her behavior:

Me: Laura, I have some important feedback to share with you. Your colleagues told me that you are argumentative with them and you don't listen to what they say. Let me give you some advice: People don't like to work for managers who are argumentative and poor listeners. If you want a promotion, you should work on your listening skills.

Laura: Who told you that?

Me: Your colleagues in the ER.

Laura: I know who you talked to. There are a few people in my unit that don't like me. That's why they told you that.

Me: It was more than just a few of your colleagues who shared that feedback with me.

Laura: Okay, but I probably just had a bad day then. My job is very stressful.

Me: I understand that your job is stressful and that you might have a bad day here and there, but this behavior is straining your relationships at work and preventing you from getting promoted.

Laura: I don't believe that. I am not argumentative and I listen well. This is the first time I am hearing this feedback. If I were argumentative, other people would have told me before now.

Notice how quickly the conversation turned into an argument about the validity of the critical feedback I was presenting. As soon as I confronted her with criticism, Laura immediately gave me reasons why the feedback wasn't accurate. Each of my rebuttals was met with another rationalization from Laura, and each round of argument-counterargument only made Laura more resistant to the critical feedback and my insistence that she needed to change her behavior.

This is usually how the script plays out when we attempt to change someone else's behavior through critical feedback or advice. We end up on opposite sides of an argument with the person we are trying to help, and in the process we make them less motivated to change and more entrenched in their denial by prompting them to come up with more arguments against change.

The reason why critical feedback and advice don't create motivation to change should be clear to you by now: They directly contradict our self-image and cause people to respond with denial and rationalization. Accepting the feedback would create uncomfortable internal tension because we would have to admit that our behavior is not consistent with our self-image *and* we would have to admit that we need to do something about it. It is much easier to just dismiss the feedback as an exception or argue why the advice wouldn't work.

Now let's see how motivational interviewing would have changed my conversation with Laura:

Me: Laura, I understand that you want to move into a management role. Is that correct?

Laura: Yes, that's what I see as the next step in my career.

Me: That is a wonderful goal. What is it about the position that interests you?

Laura: I've had so many bad managers in my career that I think I can do a much better job. Plus I've always seen myself as a leader helping my patients and my coworkers.

Me: You've had some experiences reporting to bad managers.

Laura: Yes, most of them acted like dictators, ordering people around and not really listening to their employees. And when someone would speak up, they got defensive and argumentative.

Me: These bad managers would just give you orders and they didn't listen to what you had to say. And at times they got argumentative.

Laura: Yes, exactly. I think I can do better than that.

Me: That's great. Every organization could use more good managers. Which of your strengths do you see helping you to be a good manager?

Laura: I am very open and approachable. I think it's important for people to feel comfortable around their manager and be able to talk openly about everything.

Me: You value being open and approachable and see it as an important characteristic of you being a good manager.

Laura: Yes, that's right. It makes such a big difference when your manager listens to what you have to say.

Me: Absolutely, it makes employees feel heard and appreciated. Listening is such an important skill to have as a manager. Do you always make it a point to listen to your patients and colleagues?

Laura: Yes. Well . . . sometimes when I get stressed or work gets hectic, I can be short with them.

Me: What do you mean when you say that you can be "short with them"?

Laura: Sometimes I don't have the time to listen, so I just tell them what to do.

Me: When you get stressed, or when work gets too busy, you don't listen as much.

Laura: Yes, you can say that.

Me: How often does that happen? How often do you get stressed at work?

Laura: Pretty regularly. I work in the ER, so there is always a lot going on.

Me: And when you get stressed, you tend to be short with people.

Laura: Yes, that's correct. Now that I think about it, I am stressed a lot. So I am probably not as good of a listener as I thought. Wow.

Notice how differently the second example went. When I refrained from giving Laura critical feedback or advice, I didn't trigger her resistance. We didn't get into an argument because I wasn't contradicting her self-image. Instead, I provided affirmations such as, "That is a wonderful goal," summarized what she told me, and asked her questions to guide the conversation. Through this nonthreatening process, I gently helped her to develop the internal tension between her self-image of being an open and approachable person and her behavior of being short with people. By giving her the space to explore this inconsistency on her own, I enabled her to come to the realization that she wasn't as good of a listener as she had thought. It was a positive experience rather than a fight, and Laura's transformative insight emerged from her own words, not mine. This is how motivational interviewing can help people find their motivation to change.

Motivational interviewing works in almost any situation. In a review of seventy-two scientific studies that compared the effectiveness of motivational interviewing and giving advice, motivational interviewing was found to produce better results in about 80 percent of the studies. Motivational interviewing was more effective than giving advice for weight loss, fitness, diabetes, asthma, and alcohol consumption. Moreover, even a short motivational interviewing interaction that lasted only fifteen minutes produced an effect in 64 percent of the studies.[11]

Usually when coaches and mentors first learn about motivational interviewing, they see it as a tool to try when the stakes aren't too high, and they continue to rely on critical feedback and advice in more serious cases where the stakes are high and the need for change is urgent. Don't make this mistake. If you want to help someone change, keep your advice to yourself and accept that their motivation to change has to come from within. If you try to impose it through critical feedback or advice or other confrontational methods, you will most likely start a counterproductive argument, produce resistance, and ultimately lower the person's motivation—critical feedback and advice usually end up inspiring people to come up with more reasons why they shouldn't change. Instead, use motivational interviewing as a supportive, nonconfrontational way to help others develop the internal tension that will lead them to their transformational insight.

Developing Internal Tension

At the height of the HIV/AIDS epidemic, psychologists rushed to devise interventions that would reduce the spread of the virus among sexually active adults through the use of condoms. Many government and health organizations were giving advice on condom use in the form of pamphlets, lectures, and educational videos, but by now psychologists knew that advice alone wasn't going to produce the desired behavior change. They needed to find ways to develop people's internal tension.

One such intervention pioneered during this era is called *hypocrisy induction*. Its premise is simple: You can develop internal tension in people in two steps. First you ask people to argue in favor of the desired behavior—in this case, using condoms to prevent the spread of HIV/AIDS. Then you ask them to describe situations in their recent past when they should have followed this behavior but didn't, e.g., they didn't use condoms to protect against HIV/AIDS. And just like that, the internal tension is developed and the seed of change has been planted.

In this particular experiment, college students at the University of California at Santa Cruz believed that they were helping with an HIV/AIDS prevention campaign. Specifically, they were asked to read information about the virus and use it to produce short speeches that would be shown to high school students. They recorded their speeches on video and then were asked to describe situations in their recent past when they didn't use condoms. Afterwards, the researchers administered questionnaires asking about frequency of condom use in the past and intentions to use condoms in the future.

The researchers found that students who underwent hypocrisy induction intended to use condoms more in the future. Furthermore, when researchers followed up with the study's participants three months later, they found that students in the hypocrisy induction group actually were using condoms more frequently than students who only received information about HIV/AIDS prevention.[12] In a later study, the researchers offered students the opportunity to purchase condoms immediately after they underwent hypocrisy induction, and over 80 percent of these students bought condoms; for comparison, only 30–50 percent of participants in other conditions purchased condoms.[13] Hypocrisy induction produced the motivation these students needed to change their behavior.

The hypocrisy induction technique works because it develops the internal tension people experience when their behavior is inconsistent with their self-image. The first step of the technique works to strengthen one's self-image by prompting the individual to argue in favor of something that is generally seen as desirable, such as safe driving, using condoms, or listening to employees. The same way critical feedback and advice stimulate people to come up with arguments against the change, asking people to argue for something positive stimulates them to come up with their own arguments in favor of the change. I used this technique in my second discussion with Laura when I asked her to articulate what it means to be a good manager and how her strengths would help her to be a good manager. In her responses to my questions, Laura was making the case for why good managers need to listen to their employees. By coming up with her own arguments, she solidified her opinion that active listening is an important leadership skill and connected it to her self-image as someone who wanted to be a good manager.

The second step of hypocrisy induction is trickier, because if you don't approach the subject of the person's own behavior carefully, you can create resistance and quickly spiral down to exactly the kind of futile argument you are trying to avoid. With Laura, I initiated the subject by asking an *always question*: "Do you always make it a point to listen to your patients and colleagues?" *Always* and *never* questions are useful because they are so definitive—it's unlikely that people always or never do something. Asking these types of questions is a nonthreatening way to get people to reveal their exceptions.

You can also introduce the second step of hypocrisy induction by framing it as an exploration into something you are curious about. For example, I could have said: "I am curious to understand more about how people make it a point to listen to others. Perhaps it would be easier if we explored this from the opposite side. Tell me about situations when you listened to someone less than you thought you should have."

Yet another way to introduce the second step is by asking the person about the positive attributes of a behavior. For example: "What's good about listening to your patients and coworkers?" After you explore the positive side of the behavior, then you turn the focus to the "not so good" things. For example: "What's not so good about listening to your patients and coworkers?" If you pay close attention, you can identify where someone's internal tension may lie and you go from there. Laura might have responded, "Listening to other people takes too much time when I'm busy or in the middle of a crisis," and this would have moved the conversation toward the same conclusion.

Be Patient

People must find their own motivation to change. Everyone does this in his or her own time. For some people, it happens quickly; for others, the crucial transformative insight takes longer to emerge.

Waiting for an individual to find his or her motivation can be frustrating, and you might feel pressure to speed things up by resorting to critical feedback, advice, and coercion. Don't give in to this temptation—confrontational methods will only backfire and cause the person you are trying to help to become more resistant to change. This is the opposite of what you want. Remember that your most important task as a coach or mentor helping others change their behavior is to *avoid creating resistance.* Motivational interviewing is an effective way to do this, but don't expect to be an expert at it right away. The technique is a set of complex skills that will take time for you to master and turn into habits. In the meantime, you don't have to be an expert at motivational interviewing to avoid creating resistance. When working with someone who needs to improve his or her skills, focus on listening and summarizing what the person tells you during your coaching conversations. Don't get into arguments about what he or she is doing wrong or why change is important. Instead, be patient and affirm the person's thinking. If appropriate, plant a seed of change by developing his or her internal tension. When the person is ready to change, he or she will let you know. That's your cue to begin coaching Leader Habits.

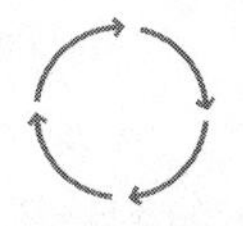

CHAPTER 9

Coaching Leader Habits

Whether you realize it or not, coaching is part of your everyday life. Any time you help other people change their behavior, whether it's your formal profession or you are a parent helping your kids build skills, you are essentially acting as a coach. You don't need a doctorate in psychology or a certificate from a coaching institute to do this. If you care about the person you are coaching and want to see him or her succeed, then you've met all the prerequisites that matter. Perhaps the learner is an employee struggling with negotiation skills or a friend who doesn't listen well. Perhaps the learner is your son, who doesn't know how to plan his school project. Or perhaps the learner is a member of your church congregation, who can't seem to build strong relationships with other people. Whatever the situation, helping others to succeed at learning new skills and behaviors is easier than you might think. You don't need to schedule formal coaching sessions every other week. You don't need to create rules and structure or formally redefine your role as the person's coach. All you need to do is pay attention to what support the person needs and then say the right thing at the right time.

If that sounds too simple, go back and read Chapter 8 again. Don't fall into the trap of thinking that it's up to you to motivate others to change. People have to come to their own insights about the need for change, and they have to find their own motivation to make change happen. If you try to force those things, you will only create resistance—you can't coerce people to learn new skills or change their behavior. All you can do is to support them through their own development journey. This is as true of leadership development as anything else.

In this chapter, I outline how to apply the Leader Habit Formula to coaching and mentoring situations. This chapter is not meant to be a comprehensive coaching guide for professional coaches and career counselors, as there are many books devoted to that topic already; instead, think of it as a primer to aid your everyday efforts as you help others develop more effective leadership habits. Most people think of leadership coaching as a structured process similar to therapy—you have regularly scheduled hour-long sessions once per month or every two weeks. For professional coaches, this model works well. But for the rest of us, coaching doesn't need a particular structure or a predefined process. We can think of coaching as a set of informal interactions: When you spend the first ten minutes of your one-on-one with an employee reflecting on his recent work assignment, you are coaching. When you encourage your daughter during dinner to continue with softball practice, you are coaching. When you talk to your congregation member after church about building stronger relationships, you are coaching. When you talk to your friend about how she could listen better, you are coaching. In everyday interactions, you have the power to impact someone's change efforts and make them more successful in building leadership skills.

In order to say the right thing at the right time, of course, you first need to know what to say, and you need to understand when to say it. That is what this chapter is about. I will outline the journey people usually undergo when applying the Leader Habit Formula, highlight how to identify where people are on their journeys, and explain what type of support they need along the way and how you can provide that support. None of this requires you to schedule formal coaching sessions. In most cases, it is best to keep your informal coaching interactions brief—a ten-minute phone call, a check-in during lunch, or a few words in passing are usually sufficient. If you are a manager embracing the Formula, you could integrate coaching discussions into your regular one-on-one meetings with your employees. If you are a parent using the Formula to teach your kids new skills, you can deliver the coaching over family dinner. And if you are using the Formula to help a friend grow, you could deliver the coaching during a hike or over a cup of tea. The point is that coaching with the Leader Habit Formula does not have to be a formal, overwhelming intervention where authority figures, friends, or family members pressure someone to change. Coaching in this context is about brief interactions that support people as they find their own way through the change process and work to develop their leadership skills by building effective Leader Habits.

Contemplating Change

Daniel had a short temper, and he knew it. What fascinated me when I worked with Daniel wasn't that he needed to learn to control his temper—plenty of people have this particular weakness—but his high degree of self-knowledge. You see, Daniel was perfectly aware that losing his temper had negative consequences, and yet he wasn't motivated to do anything to change his behavior.

Daniel was chief technology officer at a fast-growing software company, and by most measures he was a great executive. He was technically skilled, and all the developers and engineers he supervised looked up to him. He managed his teams well, showed a great deal of concern for his employees, and had a brilliant mind. He could solve complex technical and organizational problems with ease, which earned him a great reputation at the company. Professionally speaking, his only significant shortcoming was his temper.

Daniel's short temper only surfaced when he was under pressure. This isn't ideal in any industry, but if you've worked in software development, you understand why Daniel's weakness was especially problematic in his role as CTO. Deadlines and time estimates are the arch-nemesis of every developer. Most software solutions are complex, and there are many unknowns, so coming up with an accurate release date for a new software product is close to impossible. But in business, projects need deadlines. For each release cycle, Daniel would painstakingly plan the entire process, from database architecture to development and testing, but his teams would always run weeks to months behind schedule. Of course, this always created a lot of friction with other departments, especially sales and marketing, who needed to push out the new software on time to anxiously awaiting clients.

It was always toward the end of the development phase that Daniel would lose his temper, especially when he felt the pressure from his sales and marketing peers intensify. At these times, the normally calm and pleasant Daniel turned into a fire-breathing dragon. The moment he felt pushed, he got defensive and angry. There was no reasoning with him when this happened, and his colleagues on the executive team had learned not to push him when a release date was approaching. For his part, Daniel knew his outbursts were a problem, but despite his self-knowledge, the cycle kept repeating.

I always knew when Daniel was getting close to another software release: after a period of silence, he would begin calling me to talk about how stressed he was and how bad he felt about losing his temper yet again. Every time he got upset in a team meeting, he would later regret it and worry about the damage he was doing to his relationships with other executives and to his professional reputation. He would talk about how much he wished he could keep his anger under control.

I made a huge mistake during our first phone call. Excited about the successes my other clients were experiencing with the Leader Habit Formula, I proceeded to tell Daniel about how he could change his behavior with a short, 5-minute daily exercise. I assumed that his self-knowledge and willingness to talk about the negative consequences of losing his temper meant that he was ready to change his behavior. But my comments were immediately met with resistance and a laundry list of reasons why this approach would never work for him. We quickly spiraled down the argument-counterargument cycle I described in Chapter 8, and our conversation went nowhere. Only after we hung up the phone did I realize that I had misjudged the situation. Daniel knew what he was doing wrong, he knew what he needed to do differently and why, and he was willing to talk about it, but he wasn't yet ready to take action. I had to meet him where he was and offer support, not prescriptions for how to change his behavior.

With this insight, I adjusted my approach. The next time Daniel called, I just listened, summarized what he told me, and didn't offer any suggestions. When he was done sharing his regrets, I asked him how long he had been aware of the problems caused by his temper and how long he had been contemplating change. "Two years," he replied. Weeks went by, another software release came around, and Daniel rang me full of regret and worry about losing his temper again. I listened to the familiar story and kept my advice to myself. This became our routine. It went on for another six months before Daniel finally reached the point where he was ready to follow through on the changes he knew he needed to make.

Daniel's strong resistance to my initial suggestion that he use the Leader Habit Formula to change his behavior was a clear sign that he wasn't ready to take action, even though he had been thinking for years about doing something to control his temper. Self-knowledge had only brought him partway to where he needed to be. Despite understanding the problem, he was still in what psychologists call the *contemplation stage.*[1]

When people are in the contemplation stage, they are aware of their bad habits or lack of skill, and they are contemplating change. You will hear them talk about their shortcomings, and they might even express regret and worry as Daniel did. Contemplators rationally understand where they want to be, and they may even know how to get there, but they haven't yet made up their mind to take action. They are caught in a limbo of decision paralysis—they recognize the negatives of their bad behavior but also know how hard it will be to change, and they are weighing the pros and cons of committing to the challenge: "Do I care about this change enough to put in the effort? Or is it easier to stay where I am, all set and comfortable? How bad is my behavior anyway?"

A person can stay in the contemplation stage for years, as Daniel did. To contemplators, the balance between the pros and cons of changing the habit seems about even, so they don't feel enough pressure to spur them into action. It's more comfortable just to do what they have been doing, because maintaining the status quo doesn't require any extra effort. Contemplators won't take action until the scale tips and they see that the pros of changing their behavior outweigh the cons. As a coach, that is something you can help with.

Surprise the Contemplator

After years of contemplating, what finally got Daniel to move to action was when I surprised him with a question he had never considered: "What benefits do you get from losing your temper?"

It was thinking about losing his temper in terms of benefits that caught Daniel off guard. When most people attempt to influence contemplators to move to action, they focus on the negatives of the bad habit. This approach comes from the commonly held but incorrect belief that avoidance of negative consequences motivates people to change, which you learned about in Chapter 8. Most people think that if they can help tip the scale to the negative side, it will get the contemplator to act, but we know that is not the case. People don't change their habits to avoid negative consequences; they change only after they gain an insight. This is especially true for contemplators. They already know all the negative effects of their bad habits, and yet despite this knowledge about how smoking, drinking, or losing one's temper harms them, they keep doing it. Paradoxically, what contemplators need to realize is how their bad habit benefits them. What is good about smoking for the smoker? How is drinking benefiting the alcoholic? What are the positive outcomes Daniel experiences when he loses his temper? There are always benefits to be found, even in bad habits. If there weren't, the contemplator wouldn't keep doing the behavior.

Daniel didn't immediately answer my question. He had been so focused on the negatives of his habit that he couldn't come up with any benefits. I reframed the question to help him see his behavior differently. "Think of the last time that you lost your temper," I said. "What did you feel right after that happened?" Daniel recalled an executive team meeting and remembered that he had felt a sense of relief after his angry tirade. He said he had felt strong, powerful, and in control again—the opposite of how he felt when his teams were unable to deliver software on time. As we talked about that experience, he realized that he was using his anger as a way to gain control when he felt powerless. And that was the insight he needed to finally move from contemplation to action.

Once Daniel realized the benefits he gained when he lost his temper, he understood why he did it. This insight finally motivated him to change his behavior, because now he could brainstorm more effective ways to gain control and feel strong and powerful in situations that seemed to be out of his control. Now it was the right time for us to talk about the Leader Habit Formula, and we devised a simple daily exercise that taught him to control his anger.

Daniel's experience is typical for people in the contemplation stage. In a smoking-cessation program for young adults on Facebook, researchers found that "decisional balance" posts addressing both the pros and cons of smoking generated higher engagement from contemplators in the form of likes and comments than did posts that only focused on the negative aspects of smoking.[2] Like Daniel, the contemplators in this experiment knew their behavior was bad for their health; they didn't need more information about emphysema or lung cancer or any of the other cons of tobacco use. What they needed was the insight that the habit also benefited them in ways they might not have thought about before. For example, smokers may get a sense of relaxation by deeply breathing in cigarette smoke; it helps them to reduce stress. Surprising contemplators with the good things about their bad habits can lead them to important insights about why they keep engaging in those habits, and these insights can then tip the scale in favor of change. Awareness of the benefits that bad habits provide also helps people to sustain their Leader Habit practice and make their new habits permanent in the long term because they are better prepared to combat or avoid the temptations that could have them slip back into their old habits.

Substitute an Incompatible Behavior for the Bad Habit

When people think about changing their habits, they most often think of behaviors they want to stop doing, like quitting smoking, drinking less alcohol, eliminating fast food and sodas from their diet, or not losing their temper. The problem with this thinking is that it's negative—it focuses on what *not to do* rather than on what *to do*. You can't build a daily exercise on not doing something, so how do you turn this thinking around and help people find the appropriate daily exercise to practice? The answer is a simple technique that some teachers and parents are already familiar with: substitute an incompatible good behavior in place of the bad behavior.

The "stop doing that" mind-set can be hard to break because for many people the go-to strategy for correcting misbehavior is punishment. If a child is running in the lunchroom instead of walking, you yell at her to get her to stop, or you put her in time-out, or you send a note to her parents, or maybe you do all three. Next time the child runs in the lunchroom, you repeat the punishment. It's yet another instance of the familiar "change comes from avoiding negative consequences" approach to behavior modification, and it's just as ineffective as the others I've already discussed in this chapter.

The alternative to punishing a negative behavior is to reward the positive behavior you want to replace it with. The key is that the two behaviors must be *incompatible*—that is, it must be impossible for both behaviors to happen at the same time. For example, running and walking are incompatible because you can't run when you are walking, and vice versa. So instead of punishing children for running in the lunchroom, you would praise them for walking. At an elementary school in Utah, researchers tested this exact scenario. When teachers saw children walking in the lunchroom, they gave them verbal praise and a yellow note card in recognition of their good behavior; no one was punished for running. The result? Running in the lunchroom decreased by 75 percent, demonstrating that, despite popular belief, it is possible to stop undesirable behavior without punishment simply by rewarding an incompatible behavior instead.[3] This approach would prove useful for helping Daniel.

Once Daniel was ready to take action and change his short temper, I described the Leader Habit Formula to him and we looked through the catalogue of skills and exercises in Part III to find an appropriate daily exercise for him to practice. But we ran into a problem: There are no exercises targeting bad temper or controlling one's anger. We also had to find an incompatible behavior to Daniel's anger, because the Leader Habit Formula is based on adding new behaviors, rather than the old and ineffective "stop doing that" approach. Once we identified an incompatible behavior, we could build a customized Leader Habit exercise around it. I started the process with a question: "What do you see as opposite of anger?" Daniel mentioned things like caring, respect, and politeness, which matched the Leader Habit skill Show Caring. We reviewed the micro-behaviors and exercises for Show Caring, and Daniel settled on the micro-behavior "communicate with others in a polite and respectful manner." This was a good choice because Daniel couldn't angrily yell at a colleague and communicate with her in a polite and respectful manner at the same time—these two behaviors are incompatible.

Next, Daniel and I had to turn the micro-behavior into a daily exercise with an appropriate cue that would help Daniel replace the negative behavior of losing his temper with the positive behavior of communicating in a polite and respectful manner. The most effective cue for Daniel would be the moment when he first noticed that he was getting angry, because that was the moment just before he would start yelling. Daniel described feeling in these moments as if his body were a pot of boiling water with the lid on tight: The pressure built up until he erupted. We used this metaphor in our first draft of the cue: *after you notice that your body feels like a pot of boiling water.* But we still needed to turn the micro-behavior itself into a daily exercise, something Daniel could do in the moment when he started to feel angry. Given that it would be a just-in-time exercise, we had two options: either Daniel was going to make a statement or ask a question. Daniel decided to make a statement. I asked, "What would polite and respectful communication look like in this situation?" Daniel suggested that he could thank his colleagues for bringing their concerns to his attention and ask for some time to cool off before responding. And with that we had a complete first draft of Daniel's exercise to build his new Leader Habit: *After you notice that your body feels like a pot of boiling water, say, "Thank you for bringing this to my attention. Let me have a think and come back to you later."*

Our first draft of Daniel's exercise was a good start, but we still had two problems to address. The first problem was that Daniel's cue was too specific to the extreme situations where he actually lost his temper—his body felt like a pot of boiling water only when new software was coming out and when he got pushed. With a cue this specific, he wouldn't be able to practice the exercise on a daily basis, and it would be much more difficult for him to turn his new behavior into a habit. To solve this problem, we needed to find a similar cue that Daniel would encounter on a daily basis.

The second problem was that Daniel's exercise was directly tied to a strong emotional experience—getting so angry that he lost his temper. To understand why this was a problem, we need to go back to the story of my neighbor Sabrina and her dog, Max, which I introduced in Chapter 4. As you will recall, Sabrina used the technique of chaining simple behaviors together to teach Max to clean up his toys. This technique worked with all of Max's toys except one—the squeaky chicken. Max loved his squeaky chicken more than any of his other toys. Whenever the chicken squeaked, he got overwhelmed with excitement and lost his focus and started to play. Max couldn't help himself—the squeaky chicken was his emotional trigger. The excitement Max felt when the chicken squeaked prevented him from practicing his exercise and made it impossible for him to learn to put that toy away.

The problem with strong emotions like excitement for Max or anger for Daniel is that they make people (and dogs) lose their focus. Strong emotions overwhelm us, making it difficult to think rationally or concentrate on anything but the emotion itself. When it comes to building habits, strong emotions interfere with our ability to consciously practice the new behaviors we are trying to learn. If someone is replacing a bad habit that occurs in highly emotional situations, it is best to first practice dry runs of the behavior when the emotions run low. And this is exactly what Daniel did.

Although Daniel's body didn't often feel like a pot of boiling water (strong emotion), he did experience minor frustrations and irritations (weak emotion) on a daily basis, as most people do. We adjusted his exercise accordingly: *After you notice even the slightest frustration or irritation, say, "Thank you for bringing this to my attention. Let me have a think and come back to you later."* Now this exercise was something that Daniel could easily practice every day.

Supporting Leader Habit Practice

The Leader Habit Formula provides a simple action plan for people who are ready to change their behavior and develop better leadership skills: Pick a simple daily exercise and practice it until the new behavior becomes a habit. Although the Formula makes change easier, don't make the mistake of assuming that people will just cruise through their practice for sixty-six days (or longer). Expect that people will need support, formally or informally, throughout the process, and understand that different people will need different kinds of support at different times. Some people will want to publicly voice their commitment to change to you, others will look to you for confirmation that they are on the right track, others will look for an accountability partner, and yet others will need you to enhance their self-efficacy (their belief that they have the ability to succeed in making the change).

When people first start to practice an exercise, they usually seek reassurance that they are on the right track. The new behavior feels awkward and uncomfortable during this phase, so it is natural for people to need reassurance and confirmation that they are doing it right. Remember how awkward it felt when you first started buckling up in your car or picking up a new sport. Even though the Leader Habit exercises are very simple, it's unreasonable to expect that people will master them right away. Mistakes are common early in the process and shouldn't be taken as a sign of failure. As a coach, you can support the learning in getting through these early uncertainties by affirming their efforts and helping to normalize the experience. Simple statements like "most people feel awkward the first time they try a new behavior" go a long way in this regard.

New behaviors begin to feel more natural as we gain proficiency and as they become integrated into our self-image. We integrate behaviors into our self-image naturally over time—the more we do something, the more we see the behavior as part of who we are. There are also techniques you can use to help accelerate this integration. One is simply to have the learner cognitively process the experience of her practice through a brief reflection. Think of it as a follow-up to the hypocrisy induction technique you learned about in Chapter 8. In hypocrisy induction, you induce the learner to strengthen her opinion about a desirable behavior by having her argue in favor of it. This also helps the learner to identify positively with the behavior. Once the learner begins to change her behavior through deliberate practice, reflecting on the new behavior can help her to strengthen her positive identification with it and speed up the process of formulating her new self-image.

When helping people process a new experience, I recommend using a simple framework to guide the conversation. The framework I prefer is called *EAR*, which stands for "Expectation—Action—Result." EAR is a basic model for understanding human behavior. Using EAR, we can think of our everyday experiences as consisting of our expectations, our actions, and the results of those actions.

> ***Expectations*** are the thought processes that lead us to the actions we take; they include what we think about the situation we are in, any similar experiences we've had in the past, the assumptions we make, how we feel, and how we prioritize our competing needs and emotions.
>
> ***Actions*** are our actual behaviors; they consist of what we say, do, or write in response to the situation and our expectations. Actions then lead naturally to results—the outcomes of our behavior.
>
> ***Results*** include both our own reactions to what we have done and the thoughts, feelings, and behaviors of other people—what they do, say, or write in response to our actions.

You can use the EAR framework in almost any situation. In the context of the Leader Habit Formula, it is a good way to help people reflect on their first few experiences with their new exercise. Figure 9-1 provides a list of helpful questions for each part of the framework. For example, if you are using the framework to help someone reflect on their first few attempts with an exercise, you could ask about the action he or she took: "What did you do, say, or write?" Then you can explore what triggered the behavior with these questions: "What did you notice? What did you think about?" Finally, to help the learner reflect on the results of the exercise, you could ask, "What ended up happening as a result?"

At this point, it's probably helpful to see an example of how coaching support techniques actually work. Here is a conversation I had with Daniel two weeks after he started practicing his Leader Habit exercise.

Figure 9-1. Expectation–Action–Result

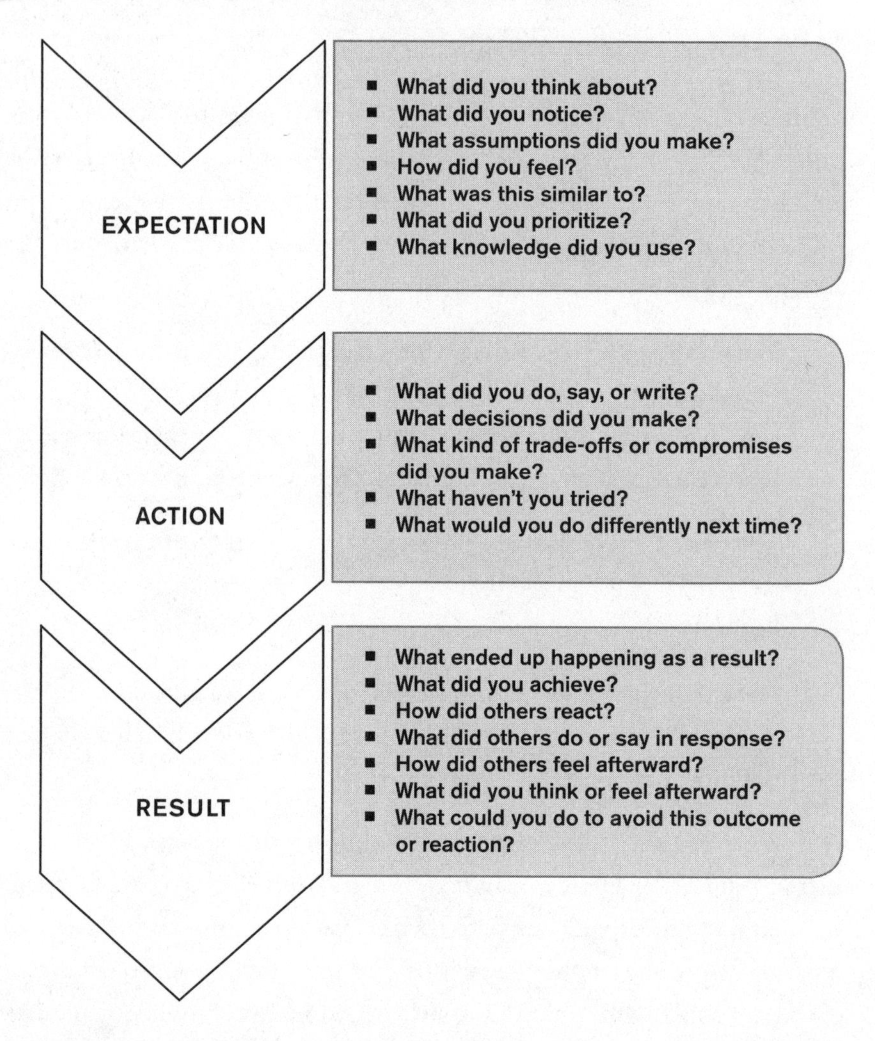

The different techniques I use are annotated with comments in square brackets.

Me: I want to check in on your exercise that we discussed last time. How is it going?

Daniel: It's going. I gave it a try on a few occasions but I must say it felt pretty strange.

Me: I am glad to hear that you tried it; that's wonderful news. ***[affirmation]*** You know, most people feel awkward when they try a new behavior. ***[normalizing the experience]***

Daniel: That's good to know. I guess anything new takes time to get comfortable.

Me: Yes, it does. I am curious to hear about how it went when you tried the exercise.

Daniel: Yesterday, I got irritated when a developer stopped me on my way home to ask me a question about a meeting. I was rushing to get out of the office to my daughter's recital and he asked me a stupid question about an agenda item for the team meeting. I felt irritated.

Me: What did you do? ***[action]***

Daniel: I thanked him for bringing it to my attention and told him that I would get back to him later.

Me: That's great! You had a great opportunity to practice the exercise and you remembered to do that. ***[affirmation]***

Daniel: Yes, I did.

Me: What happened as a result? ***[result]***

Daniel: He said, "Okay, thanks."

Me: How did you feel after that? ***[result]***

Daniel: It actually made me feel good. I didn't get angry, yell at him, or dismiss his question. It was good practice.

Me: You acknowledged his question and told him that you would get back to him later. You showed up as a polite, respectful person. ***[summarizing]***

Daniel: Yes. It made me feel good.

Me: Excellent. I am glad to hear that. What did you think before he stopped you? ***[expectation]***

Daniel: I was rushing out of the office as I was afraid that I would be late to my daughter's recital.

Me: What did you think about his question? ***[expectation]***

Daniel: I thought that it was stupid. He saw that I was in a hurry and he could have just looked up the meeting agenda. He didn't have to stop me.

Me: You made the assumption that he recognized you rushing out and so you found his question disrespectful. ***[summarizing]***

Daniel: You could say that, yes.

Me: Is that why you felt irritated? ***[expectation]***

Daniel: Yes, I was clearly in a hurry and he should have noticed that.

Me: What made you think of the exercise? ***[exploring the cue]***

Daniel: It was the irritation—I was afraid I was going to be late and he stopped me with a trivial question.

Notice how I reinforced Daniel's first attempts at practicing the exercise and normalized his experience by saying that other people feel awkward when they first try something new. I also used the EAR framework to get him to reflect on his experience of the exercise. I helped him to explore the action he took, what triggered the action, and the result of that action. Then we focused on the cue, specifically how he recognized it and what made him think to deliberately practice the exercise. The goal of this simple coaching discussion was to reinforce Daniel's attempts with affirmations and to solidify his practice by strengthening his self-image as a polite and respectful person. By encouraging him to think through the cue and identify its characteristics, I made it more likely that Daniel would recognize similar situations in the future and continue to practice his behavior.

"You Can Do It"

If a learner's first few attempts with his Leader Habit exercise are positive, he will be more likely to continue practicing the exercise. As you saw in my conversation with Daniel, creating a comfortable space where the learner can reflect on his experiences with the exercise is a good way to do this. Another powerful technique to support Leader Habit practice is to increase the learner's self-efficacy—his belief that he can continue practicing and succeed in learning his new behavior.

One of the most common coaching techniques assumed to increase self-efficacy is helping the learner identify the barriers to success that stand in his or her path of change. We have been taught to do this as a way to help people to reflect on what's preventing them from accomplishing their goals, so they can find ways to overcome those barriers. You know the questions: What's standing in your way? What's preventing you from doing *x*? What barriers do you see in *y*?

These questions are well intended, but they backfire: A review of twenty-seven research studies that attempted to increase people's self-efficacy found that the technique of identifying and discussing barriers actually resulted in *lower* self-efficacy.[4] After exploring their personal barriers, people have *less* belief in their ability to succeed. This makes sense if you understand why critical feedback doesn't work to motivate people to change. In the same way that critical feedback causes people to actively come up with arguments against change, asking people to think about the barriers they face causes them to come up with reasons why they can't succeed. If you use this technique with people who want to improve their leadership skills, they will tell you all the reasons why they can't practice their Leader Habit exercise or why the change is too hard—and in the process, they will probably convince themselves that these reasons are true. So what should you do instead?

The same research review identified several tactics that are effective at increasing self-efficacy. First, positive persuasion techniques like building up a person's confidence or focusing on the benefits of the change do make a difference. It never hurts to tell someone, "You can do this! Keep practicing, it will make you a better leader." But don't stop at positive persuasion. The technique that increases self-efficacy the most is something else: letting people know how much they have already practiced.[5] This explains the findings of the pedometer study I described in Chapter 5, in which participants who were able to track their performance on their smartphones logged more physical activity than those who didn't have access to the phone app.[6] Monitoring their past performance made these participants aware of their successes—they could see how many steps they had taken. Simply seeing what they had already achieved made them believe they could achieve more, which in turn encouraged them to actually *do* more.

Making people aware of their successes is a simple and effective way to increase their self-efficacy. Even a few successful early attempts at a Leader Habit exercise can become the foundation for a learner's belief in her own ability to improve her leadership skills.

Interestingly, the research review also found that providing written feedback on people's past practice (either via email or online) produced higher self-efficacy than offering the same feedback verbally.[7] It is therefore important that you encourage others to track their practice in written form, as I recommended in Chapter 5. Some ideas for written tracking include crossing off days in a paper calendar, checking off recurring tasks or to-dos, or using a habit-tracking smartphone application. The more rigorously people track their practice, the more the feedback will boost their self-efficacy. Tracking also provides opportunities for simple coaching discussions about past successes. For example, you can ask how many total days a learner has practiced, or what her longest streak of consecutive days of practice is. And you can use this information to help her celebrate her early wins: "You practiced for ten days already! That's a great accomplishment."

In addition to identifying the effectiveness of tracking practice as a way to increase self-efficacy, the research review found another technique that works almost as well: having learners observe how other people enact the behavior they are practicing.[8] It turns out that seeing others do something makes us believe that we can do it, too, thus increasing our self-efficacy. For example, you could model the Leader Habit exercise for your learner, or you could have him observe other people who have already mastered the skill. Afterward, use the EAR framework in Figure 9-1 to discuss what he learned from the observation. Try posing questions like: What was the situation? What triggered the person to do this behavior? What exactly did the person do? What were the results of that behavior? How did other people react to it? What was the outcome for you—what did you think and how did you feel?

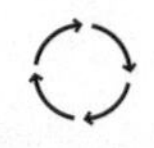

Don't Stop Now

As people progress in their Leader Habit practice and gain competency in their new behavior, their improving skill becomes apparent to others and it may seem as though they have successfully turned the behavior into a habit. In most cases this happens when the learner is approaching or has achieved mastery, which is well before the habit is actually formed. This is a crucial point in the learner's development. Once she reaches mastery, it will seem like there's nothing more she can learn, and she will feel a strong temptation to stop practicing her Leader Habit exercise. But remember that automaticity, the key to habit-formation, happens only during the over-learning phase, when people continue to practice an exercise *beyond* mastery. The danger here is that all the effort the learner has put in up to this point will be wasted if she stops practicing now and doesn't turn the behavior into a habit. The support you offer during this phase must be focused on helping the learner continue her practice until the habit is truly formed. As soon as you notice that the person you are coaching has reached mastery, it is time to revisit the concept of automaticity and begin managing expectations about when the learner can expect her habit to be fully formed. You will know the learner has reached mastery when she can do the exercise flawlessly, when she is confident about performing the exercise, and when she begins to feel like she can't get any better. This is a good opportunity to use the Automaticity Checklist (Figure 2-1) in Chapter 2 to see whether automaticity has begun to form.

Managing expectations for a learner who has reached mastery is all about reminding her how long it takes to form a habit—sixty-six days of practice on average (and possibly longer, depending on the person and the behavior in question).[9] Even people who understand the Leader Habit Formula perfectly well in theory have trouble accepting the sixty-six-day baseline in practice, perhaps because it is more than three times longer than the popular belief that it takes only twenty-one days to form a habit. I have found that it helps to explain how the learner's brain has created a mental model of the behavior that resulted in mastery. Now, during the over-learning phase, continuing to practice is causing her brain to work hard to update this mental model by cutting out unnecessary processes and eliminating energy waste. The learner is not consciously aware of her brain working hard at this stage because achieving mastery has made the behavior seem easy to her, but internally that is what is happening, and all this unconscious hard work is what turns the behavior into a habit. If the learner stops practicing before the mental model is completely refined, the habit won't form. This is why the learner *must* continue to practice, even though it feels like she can't get any better at the exercise.

Supporting Habit-Building Efforts

As I wrote at the beginning of this chapter, coaching to Leader Habits is about providing the support people need as they work through the process of developing new leadership skills. This support can be formal or informal, depending on the situation. Either way, it all comes down to saying the right thing at the right time. If you need a quick reference to help you prepare for your coaching interactions, Figure 9-2 illustrates the different stages people go through as they develop Leader Habits, lists the key indicators that correspond to each stage, and offers suggestions for how to support people in each stage.

Always remember that people start the development journey on their own terms and in their own time, when they are ready to do so. People who are unaware of their bad habits or lack of skill and who show resistance to feedback probably are not ready for change. You can't motivate them with criticism or threats of negative consequences or anything external; the motivation to change must come from within. At this

Figure 9-2. Coaching Leader Habits

Not ready
- Unaware of shortcomings and resists feedback
- Develop internal tension

↓

Contemplating
- Aware of shortcomings and considering change
- Surprise by asking about benefits of bad behavior

↓

Ready for action
- Committed to change
- Explain the Leader Habit Formula and find the best exercise

↓

Early attempts
- First two weeks of practice
- Facilitate reflection using EAR framework

↓

Practicing
- Continued practice after early attempts
- Increase self-efficacy by discussing past successful practice
- Continue with reflections using EAR framework

↓

Over-learning
- Reached mastery—flawless performance
- Check on automaticity
- Manage expectations

stage it's best to help people develop the internal tension between their self-image and their actual behavior. Bringing such inconsistency into a person's conscious awareness can create the insight that will motivate him or her to start a development journey.

People who understand the need to change don't always begin the process right away; often they must contemplate the change and convince themselves that it is worth the effort. At this stage they are aware of their problem behavior or lack of skill and are seriously considering taking action. They weigh the pros and cons of the change—how bad is the bad behavior, how important is the new skill, how much energy are they willing to devote to the change effort, and so on. When a person is in the contemplation stage, the pros and cons of change appear to her or him to be evenly balanced. The scale needs to tip one way or the other for her to take action; otherwise, she will stay in the contemplation stage. Tipping the scales is something you can help with. Instead of focusing on the negative aspects of a person's behavior, surprise him by helping him understand what benefits he is getting from it. This shift in perspective can help a person break the paralysis of contemplation and move to action.

When someone is ready for action—let's say her name is Diane—she is committed to change. It is difficult to know for sure that Diane has reached this stage until she makes her initial attempts at change. But if she lets you know that she is ready to change her behavior, that's usually a good sign. At this point it is important to develop a simple, clear action plan, and that's where the Leader Habit Formula comes in. I recommend taking some time to briefly explain to Diane how the Formula works and the research behind it, as this helps to create buy-in. Then work with her, as the learner, to help her find her first Leader Habit exercise in Part III.

After Diane has settled on her first exercise, the work of deliberate practice begins. I recommend that you set up a tracking mechanism immediately, so that she can monitor her practice. The exercise will most likely feel awkward at first, so Diane needs affirmations that she is on the right track. Use the EAR framework in Figure 9-1 to help her process her early attempts at the exercise to reassure her that she is doing it right or to identify adjustments that will make the exercise more effective for her. Maybe the cue needs to be more salient, or the behavior smaller.

If the early attempts go well and Diane is reassured that she is on the right track, she will continue to practice. At this stage, as she learns she will continue to seek reassurance and affirmation of her efforts. You can support her by increasing her self-efficacy and periodically highlighting past successful practice. Such affirmations will reassure her that she can be successful and motivate her to sustain her practice. It is also useful to continue with periodic reflections to ensure that you both understand what is working well and what needs adjusting.

The beauty of the Leader Habit Formula is that behavioral change tends to happen quickly and people soon achieve mastery of their exercise. At this point, the over-learning phase of the habit cycle begins. During the over-learning phase, people will be able to do the exercises flawlessly. This is a significant accomplishment, but it can create problems if the learners don't understand the need to continue practicing beyond mastery, since they may be feeling like they are stagnating and it's time to move on to a new exercise. To coach people through over-learning, use the Automaticity Checklist (Figure 2-1 in Chapter 2) to see how close they are to forming a habit, and manage their expectations by reiterating that it takes an average of sixty-six days of practice to achieve automaticity.[10] It may also help to explain how their brains are unconsciously working hard to streamline their mental model of the behavior, even though the exercise no longer seems to require much conscious effort.

Keep in mind that while I have described developing leadership skills with the Leader Habit Formula as a linear process, it is not uncommon for people to circle back to an earlier stage, especially when they encounter setbacks. Therefore don't assume that the learners you are coaching are only moving forward. You must remain vigilant at all times to see where they are in the process and adjust your support accordingly.

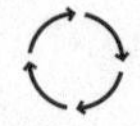

Leading Lives with Habits

The Leader Habit Formula provides a handy model you can use to help others develop leadership skills and to become a better leader and coach yourself. The model is easy to explain, and the catalogue of leadership skills and exercises provided in Part III makes it easy to put into practice. Parents, teachers, friends, church and community leaders, and informal mentors can use these principles to help others achieve personal growth. Corporate managers can use the Formula to develop their employees; executive and life coaches and consultants can use it with their clients; and Human Resources and Organizational Development professionals can use it to build effective leadership development programs within their organizations.

Life changes constantly, yet we bring our habitual responses with us to every situation we encounter, for better or for worse. Every new conscious behavior you engage in today has the potential to become a new habit. Some of these habits you will appreciate; others you will regret. Once a habit forms, you may not remember intentionally starting it, but you surely will have a hard time breaking it. Such is the power of our brain's ability to turn behaviors into automatic responses to specific cues. This power can hold us back if our habits are negative, or it can help us grow if we use it to develop new skills. This is true whether you are building your own habits or supporting the habit-building efforts of others. Who you consciously decide to be today is the person you will automatically be in just a few months, after your new habits take root and begin shaping your actions through new unconscious behaviors. Use this power to your advantage. The Leader Habit Formula gives you and anyone you coach the ability to easily master the skills you need to lead in just minutes a day. The sooner you start practicing, the sooner you will see the change—and the sooner your new skills will become your Leader Habits.

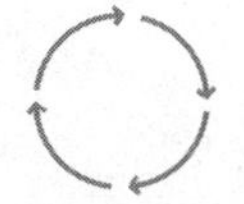

ACKNOWLEDGEMENTS

This book was a team effort. I would like to recognize the brilliant team at AMACOM, who made the publishing process a wonderfully fulfilling experience, and my exquisite team at Pinsight® who puts up with my good and bad leadership habits on a daily basis. A number of people made significant contributions to this book, either directly or by influencing my thinking, business, and life. Special thanks to:

Mark Springer for tirelessly revising, editing, and commenting on every chapter, section, page, and sentence. You gave the content style.

Ellen Kadin for giving me the opportunity to resubmit my proposal five times. I'm keeping my fingers crossed that the last version works.

Jennifer Holder for suggesting I rewrite a third of this book over Labor Day weekend. I believe it made the book (and me) stronger.

Christy Panico, Bernie Voss, and everyone else at Pinsight® who contributed to our global research study on leadership skills. Let's hope our insights make bad managers disappear.

Laura, Scott, my neighbor Sabrina, Max the golden retriever, John, Ruth, and Daniel. I will never reveal who is who in real life.

My mother for encouraging me to get on the plane back to the United States when I wanted to quit, my sister for always laughing with me, and my grandma for letting me use her typewriter for my very first book (that I hope no one ever finds). I love you all dearly.

Bob and Jeanne Endsley for teaching me the habit of generosity.

Tara Vega for answering WhatsApp messages at 3:00 a.m. You've got to stop that!

Miles Baldwin for helping me turn a graduate-school project into a thriving business.

Christine and Jacques Devaud for the stimulating business discussions around your perfectly set table.

Lee Kooler, whose last name should really be "koolest," because during her class I fell in love with psychology.

Jamie McCreary for introducing me to my future career in consulting.

Kurt Kraiger and George Thornton for patiently supervising my graduate work.

Dasa Pikalova and Alejandro Sabre who taught me the discipline of daily (piano) practice.

Autumn and Tess. You see my bad habits more clearly than anyone and yet you're still my friends.

And finally, thanks to our corporate clients, who continue to invest in developing their people, and the thousands of aspiring leaders around the world who complete our programs every year. Your new habits continue to inspire all of us at Pinsight®.

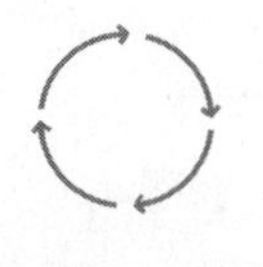

NOTES

Chapter One

1. Wendy Wood and David T. Neal, "The habitual consumer," *Journal of Consumer Psychology* 19, no. 4 (2009): 580, doi: 10.1016/j.jcps.2009.08.003.
2. Frederico A. C. Azevedo, Ludmila R. B. Carvalho, Leat T. Grinberg, Jose M. Farfel, Renata E. L. Ferretti, Renata E. P. Leite, Wilson J. Filho, Roberto Lent, and Suzana Herculana-Houzel, "Equal numbers of neuronal and nonneuronal cells make the human brain an isometrically scaled-up primate brain," *The Journal of Comparative Neurology* 513, no. 5 (2009): 532, doi: 10.1002/cne.21974.
3. John A. Bargh, Mark Chen, and Lara Burrows, "Automaticity of Social Behavior: Direct Effects of Trait Construct and Stereotype Activation on Action," *Journal of Personality and Social Psychology* 71, no. 2 (1996): 230–244, doi: 10.1037/0022-3514.71.2.230.
4. David T. Neal, Wendy Wood, Jennifer S. Labrecque, and Phillippa Lally, "How do habits guide behavior? Perceived and actual triggers of habits in daily life," *Journal of Experimental Social Psychology* 48, no. 2 (2012): 492–498, doi: 10.1016/j.jesp.2011.10.011.
5. John A. Bargh and Tanya L. Chartrand, "The Unbearable Automaticity of Being," *American Psychologist* 54, no. 7 (1999): 462–479, doi: 10.1037/0003-066X.54.7.462.
6. Jeffrey M. Quinn and Wendy Wood, "Habits Across the Lifespan" (working paper, Duke University, 2005), 12.
7. Wendy Wood, Jeffrey M. Quinn, and Deborah A. Kashy, "Habits in Everyday Life: Thought, Emotion, and Action," *Journal of Personality and Social Psychology* 83, no. 6 (2002): 1286, doi: 10.1037/0022-3514.83.6.1281.
8. Fermin Moscoso Del Prado Martin, "The thermodynamics of human reaction times," retrieved from https://arxiv.org/pdf/0908.3170.pdf (August 2009), 6.
9. Beth Crandall and Karen Gethcell-Reiter, "Human Factors in Medicine: Critical Decision Method: A Technique for Eliciting Concrete Assessment Indicators from the Intuition of NICU Nurses," *Advances in Nursing Science* 16, no. 1 (1993): 72–77.

10. Milan Kundera, *The Unbearable Lightness of Being* (New York: Harper & Row, 1984).
11. Richard D. Arvey, Maria Rotundo, Wendy Johnson, Zhen Zhang, and Matt McGue, "The determinants of leadership role occupancy: Genetic and personality factors," *The Leadership Quarterly* 17, no. 1 (2006): 1, doi: 10.1016/j.leaqua.2005.10.009.
12. Anoop K. Patiar and Lokman Mia, "Transformational Leadership Style, Market Competition and Departmental Performance: Evidence from Luxury Hotels in Australia," *International Journal of Hospitality Management* 28, no. 2 (2009): 259, doi: 10.1016/j.ijhm.2008.09.003.
13. Rod L. Flanigan, Gary Stewardson, Jeffrew Dew, Michelle M. Fleig-Palmer, and Edward Reeve, "Effects of Leadership on Financial Performance at the Local Level of an Industrial Distributor," *The Journal of Technology, Management, and Applied Engineering* 29, no. 4 (2013): 6–7.
14. John LaRosa, "Overview & Status of The U.S. Self-improvement Market: Market Size, Segments, Emerging Trends & Forecasts," *Market Data Enterprises Inc.*, November 2013, https://www.slideshare.net/jonlar/the-us-self-improvement-market
15. Andrea Derler, "Boosted Spend on Leadership Development—The Facts and Figures," *Bersin by Deloitte* (blog), July 18, 2012, http://blog.bersin.com/boosted-spend-on-leadership-development-the-facts-and-figures/
16. Robert B. Kaiser and Gordy Curphy, "Leadership Development: The Failure of an Industry and the Opportunity for Consulting Psychologists," *Consulting Psychology Journal: Practice and Research* 65, no. 4 (2013): 294, doi: 10.1037/a0035460.
17. Laci Loew, *State of Leadership Development in 2015: The Time to Act is Now* (Brandon Hall Group, 2015), 5. PDF e-book, http://www.ddiworld.com/DDI/media/trend-research/state-of-leadership-development_tr_brandon-hall.pdf?ext=.pdf%25252520
18. Lindsay Thomson, Lauretta Lu, Deanna Pate, Britt Andreatta, Allison Schnidman, and Todd Dewett, *2017 Workplace Learning Report: How modern L&D pros are tackling top challenges*, (LinkedIn, 2017), 17. PDF e-book, https://learning.linkedin.com/content/dam/me/learning/en-us/pdfs/lil-workplace-learning-report.pdf
19. David L. Georgensen, "The problem of transfer calls for partnership," *Training and Development Journal* 36, no. 10 (1982): 75–78.
20. Alfred H. Fuchs and Katharine S. Milar, "Psychology as a Science," *Handbook of Psychology Volume I: History of Psychology*, eds. Donald Freedheim and Irving Weiner (John Wiley & Sons, 2003), 6. PDF e-book, http://areas.fba.ul.pt/jpeneda/Psychology%20as%20a%20Science.pdf
21. Harry P. Bahrick, Lorraine E. Bahrick, Audrey S. Bahrick, and Phyllis E. Bahrick, "Maintenance of Foreign Language Vocabulary and the Spacing Effect," *Psychological Science* 4, no. 5 (1993): 318–319, doi: 10.1111/j.1467-9280.1993.tb00571.x.

Chapter Two

1. Pamela Engel, "Heroic Flight Attendant Was The Last Person To Leave The Burning Asiana Flight 214," Transportation, *Business Insider*, Jul. 9, 2013, http://www.businessinsider.com/lee-yoon-hye-rescues-passengers-on-asiana-flight-214-2013-7
2. Phillippa Lally, Cornelia H. M. van Jaarsveld, Henry W. W. Potts, and Jane Wardle, "How are habits formed: Modelling habit formation in the real world," *European Journal of Social Psychology* 40, no. 6 (2009): 1002, doi:10.1002/ejsp.674.
3. Helen J. Huang, Rodger Kram, and Alaa A. Ahmed, "Reduction of Metabolic Cost during Motor Learning of Arm Reaching Dynamics," *The Journal of Neuroscience* 32, no. 6 (2012): 2186–2187, doi:10.1523/JNEUROSCI.4003-11.2012.
4. Burrhus F. Skinner, "'Superstition' in the Pidgeon," *Journal of Experimental Psychology* 38, no. 2 (1948), 168–172, doi:10.1037/h0055873.
5. Andrew C. Peck and Mark C. Detweiler, Training Concurrent Multistep Procedural Tasks," *Human Factors* 42, no. 3 (2000): 386–387, doi:10.1518/001872000779698150.
6. Wendy Wood, Jeffrey M. Quinn, and Deborah A. Kashy, "Habits in Everyday Life: Thought, Emotion, and Action," *Journal of Personality and Social Psychology* 83, no. 6 (2002): 1292, doi:10.1037//0022-3514.83.66.1281.
7. Wendy Wood and David T. Neal, "A New Look at Habits and the Habit-Goal Interface," *Psychological Review* 114, no. 4 (2007): 858, doi:10.1037/0033-295X.114.4.843.
8. David T. Neal, Wendy Wood, Phillippa Lally, and Mengju Wu, "Do Habits Depend on Goals? Perceived versus Actual Role of Goals in Habit Performance" (unpublished, Research Gate 2009), 23–28.
9. Richard L. Marsh, Jason L. Hicks, and Thomas W. Hancock, "On the Interaction of Ongoing Cognitive Activity and the Nature of an Event-Based Intention," *Applied Cognitive Psychology* 14, no. 7 (2000): 833–836, doi: 10.1002/acp.769.
10. Bas Verplanken, "Beyond frequency: Habit as mental construct," *British Journal of Social Psychology* 45, no. 3 (2006), 639–656, doi:10.1348/014466605X49122.
11. David Montero, "Utah officials celebrate 100th anniversary of traffic signal," *Salt Lake Tribune*, Oct. 4, 2012, http://archive.sltrib.com/story.php?ref=/sltrib/politics/55027680-90/1912-green-invention-lake.html.csp
12. See note 7 above.
13. Matthew M. Botvinick and Lauren M. Bylsma, "Distraction and action slips in an everyday task: Evidence for a dynamic representation of task context," *Psychonomic Bulletin & Review* 12, no. 6 (2005): 1014–1015, doi: 10.3758/BF03206436.
14. Marketdata Enterprises, "Weight Loss Market Sheds Some Dollars in 2013," Press Release (Feb. 2014), retrieved from: https://www

.marketdataenterprises.com/wp-content/uploads/2014/01/Diet-Market-2014-Status-Report.pdf
15. International Health, Racquet & Sportsclub Association, "IHRSA Trend Report" (Jan. 2014), retrieved from: http://www.ihrsa.org/consumer-research/
16. Maxwell Maltz, *Psycho-Cybernetics* (Englewood Cliffs, NJ: Prentice-Hall, 1960), xiii.
17. See note 2 above.
18. Lee N. Robins, "Vietnam veterans' rapid recovery from heroin addiction: a fluke or normal expectation?" *Addiction* 88, no. 8 (1993): 1041–1054, doi: 10.1111/j.1360-0443.1993.tb02123.x.
19. Dan Ariely, *What makes us feel good about our work?* TED Talk Video, 20:26, October 2012, https://www.ted.com/talks/dan_ariely_what_makes_us_feel_good_about_our_work?language=en
20. Kaitlin Woolley and Ayelet Fishbach, "The Experience Matters More Than You Think: People Value Intrinsic Incentives More Inside Than Outside an Activity," *Journal of Personality and Social Psychology* 109, no. 6, 972, doi: 10.1037/pspa0000035.
21. Charles A. O'Reilly III, "Personality-job fit: Implications for individual attitudes and performance," *Organizational Behavior and Human Performance* 18, no. 1 (1977): 36-46, doi: 10.1016/0030-5073(77)90017-4.

Chapter Three

1. Tristan Pang, "Quest is fun, be nosey: Tristan Pang at TEDxYouth@Auckland," YouTube video, 8:22, from TEDxYouth@Aukland on October 26, 2013, posted by "TEDxYouth," November 13, 2013, https://www.youtube.com/watch?v=sbMKX4J03nY
2. Tristan Pang, "The Future of Education: but not as you know it," *QUEST IS FUN*, March 4, 2014, accessed August 18, 2017, http://quest-is-fun.org.nz/author/tristan/
3. See note 1 above.
4. Mihály Csíkszentmihályi, *Flow: The Psychology of Optimal Experiences* (New York: Harper and Row, 1990).
5. Mihály Csíkszentmihályi, "Flow, the Secret to Happiness," *TED.com*, 18:55, from TED2004 on February 27, 2004, https://www.ted.com/talks/mihaly_csikszentmihalyi_on_flow?language=en
6. Timoner, "Flow State: How to Cultivate a State of Bliss and Seamless Productivity," *The Blog* (blog), *Huffington Post*, January 27, 2014, http://www.huffingtonpost.com/ondi-timoner/flow-genome-project-how-t_b_4652235.html
7. Kenneth Kushner and Jackson Morisawa, *One arrow, One Life: Zen, Archery, Enlightenment* (Singapore: Tuttle Publishing, 2000).
8. Chan Wing-tsit, Chu Ron Guey, Dardess John, Farmer Edward, Hurvitz Leon, Keightley David N., Lynn Richard John, Nivison David S., Queen

Sarah, Roth Harold, Schirokauer Conrad, Sivin Nathan, Stevenson Daniel, Verellen Franciscus, Watson Burton, Yampolsky Philip B., Yü Chün-fang, Adler Joseph, Amster Martin, Bielefeldt Carl, Birdwhistell Anne, Birge Bettine, Chan Hok-lam, Ching Julia, Ch'ü T'ung-tsu, Dien Albert, Ebrey Patricia B., Foulk T. Griffith, Gentzler J. Mason, Guarino Marie, Hartman Charles, Hymes Robert, Johnson Wallace, Kelleher Theresa, Kwok Daniel W. Y., Lee Thomas H. C., Shu-hsien Liu, Meskill John T., Orzech Charles D., Owen Stephen, Schipper Kristofer, Smith Joanna Handlin, Smith Kidder, Tanabe George, Tillman Hoyt, Heng-ting Tsai, and Weiming Tu, "THE WAY OF LAOZI AND ZHUANGZI," in *Sources of Chinese Tradition: Volume 1: From Earliest Times to 1600*, eds. Theodore De Bary and Irene Bloom (New York: Columbia University Press, 1999), 103.

9. Mihály Csíkszentmihályi and Olga V. Beattie, "Life Themes: A Theoretical and Empirical Exploration of Their Origins and Effects," *Journal of Humanistic Psychology* 19, no. 1 (1979): 45–63, doi: 10.1177/002216787901900105; Mihály Csíkszentmihályi and Jeremy Hunter, "Happiness in Everyday Life: The Uses of Experience Sampling," *Journal of Happiness Studies* 4, no. 2 (2003): 185–199, doi: 10.1023/A:1024409732742; Mihály Csíkszentmihályi and Judith LeFevre, "Optimal Experience in Work and Leisure," *Journal of Personality and Social Psychology* 56, no. 5 (1989): 815–822, doi: 10.1037/0022-3514.56.5.815; Jeanne Nakamura and Mihály Csíkszentmihályi, "The Construction of Meaning Through Vital Engagement," in *Flourishing: Positive Psychology and the Life Well-Lived*, eds. Corey Keyes and Jonathan Haidt (Washington, District of Columbia: American Psychological Association, 2003), 83–104.
10. Sointu Leikas, Jan-Erik Lönnqvist, and Markku Verkasalo, "Persons, Situations, and Behaviors: Consistency and Variability of Different Behaviors in Four Interpersonal Situations," *Journal of Personality and Social Psychology* 103, no. 6 (2012): 1007–1022, doi: 10.1037/a0030385.
11. Bella M. DePaulo, Amy L. Blank, Gregory W. Swaim, and Joan G. Hairfield, "Expressiveness and Expressive Control," *Personality and Social Psychology Bulletin* 18, no. 3 (1992): 276–285, doi: 10.1177/0146167292183003.
12. Sir Francis Galton, "The Measurement of Character," *Fortnightly Review* 42 (1884): 179–185.
13. Michael C. Ashton and Kibeom Lee, "The prediction of Honesty-Humility-related criteria by the HEXACO and Five-Factor Models of personality," *Journal of Research in Personality* 42, no. 5 (2008): 1216–1228, doi: j.jrp.2008.03.006; Michael C. Ashton, Kibeom Lee, Marco Perugini, Piotr Szarota, Reinout E. de Vries, Lisa Di Blas, Kathleen Boies, and Boele De Raad, "A Six-Factor Structure of Personality-Descriptive Adjectives: Solutions from Psycholexical Studies in Seven Languages,"

Journal of Personality and Social Psychology 86, no. 2 (2004): 356–366, doi: 10.1037/0022-3514.86.2.356; Raymond B. Cattell, *The Scientific Use of Factor Analysis* (New York: Plenum Press, 1978); Mark H. Do, Amirali Minbashian, "A meta-analytic examination of the effects of agentic and affiliative aspects of extraversion on leadership outcomes," *The Leadership Quarterly* 25, no. 5 (2014): 1046–1047, doi: 10.1016/j.leaqua.2014.04.004.

14. Stephan Dilchert and Deniz S. Ones, "Assessment Center Dimensions: Individual differences correlates and meta-analytic incremental validity," *International Journal of Selection and Assessment* 17, no. 3 (2009): 260, doi: j.1468-2389.2009.00468.x.
15. Hege Kornør and Hilmar Nordvik, "Personality traits in leadership behavior," *Scandinavian Journal of Psychology* 45, no.1 (2004): 51–52, doi: 10.1111/j.1467-9450.2004.00377.x.
16. See note 14 above.
17. See note 15 above.
18. See note 14 above.
19. Robert B. Kaiser and Joyce Hogan, "Personality, Leader Behavior, and Overdoing It," *Consulting Psychology Journal: Practice and Research* 63, no. 4 (2011): 226–230, doi: 10.1037/a0026795.
20. See note 15 above.
21. See note 15 above.
22. See note 15 above.
23. See note 14 above.
24. José Navarro, Fernando Curioso, Duarte Gomes, Carlos Arrieta, and Maricio Cortés, "Fluctuations in Work Motivation: Tasks do not Matter!" *Nonlinear Dynamics, Psychology, and Life Sciences* 17, no. 1 (2013): 8–15.
25. Shuhua Sun, Jeffrey B. Vancouver, and Justin M. Weinhardt, "Goal choices and planning: Distinct expectancy and value effects in two goal processes," *Organizational Behavior and Human Decision Processes* 125, no. 2 (2014): 224–226, doi: 10.1016/j.obhdp.2014.09.002.
26. Albert Ellis and William J. Knaus, *Overcoming Procrastination* (New York: Institute for Rational Living, 1977); William K. O'Brien, "Applying the Transtheoretical Model to Academic Procrastination" (Doctoral Dissertation, University of Houston, 2002); Timothy J. Potts, "Predicting Procrastination on Academic Tasks with Self-report Personality Measures" (doctoral dissertation, Hofstra University, 1987).
27. Robert M. Klassen, Lindsey L. Krawchuk, and Sukaina Rajani, "Academic procrastination of undergraduates: Low self-efficacy to self-regulate predicts higher levels of procrastination," *Contemporary Educational Psychology* 33, no. 4 (2008): 919–922, doi: 10.1016/j.cedpsych.2007.07.001.
28. Chip Heath and Dan Heath, *Switch: How to Change Things When Change Is Hard* (New York: Crown Business, 2010), 130–131.

Chapter Four

1. Pamela Johnson, "Using Back Chaining to Train Tricks, Dog Sports and Real World Behaviors–Pamela Johnson," YouTube video, 7:04, Tawzer Dog LLC, posted by "Tawzer Dog," September 11, 2015, https://www.youtube.com/watch?v=5vPqMk5Z6J8
2. Fred Spooner, Doreen Spooner, and Gary Ulicny, "Comparisons of Modified Backward Chaining: Backward Chaining with Leap-aheads and Reverse Chaining with Leap-aheads," *Education and Treatment of Children* 9, no. 2 (1986): 123.
3. Charles Duhigg, *The Power of Habit* (New York: Random House, 2012), 108–109.
4. Albert Bandura, *Self-efficacy: The exercise of control* (New York: Freeman, 1997).
5. Chip Heath and Dan Heath, *Switch: How to Change Things When Change Is Hard* (New York: Crown Business, 2010), 130–131.
6. D. R. Godden and A. D. Baddeley, "Context-dependent Memory in Two Natural Environments: On Land and Underwater," *British Journal of Psychology* 66, no. 3 (1975): 325–331, doi: 10.1111/j.2044-8295.1975.tb01468.x.
7. Timothy D. Ludwig and E. Scott Geller, "Improving the Driving Practices of Pizza Deliverers: Response Generalization and Moderating Effects of Driving History," *Journal of Applied Behavior Analysis* 24, no. 1 (1991): 32–41, doi: 10.1901/jaba.1991.24-31.
8. Jonathan L. Freedman and Scott C. Fraser, "Compliance Without Pressure: The Foot-In-The-Door Technique," *Journal of Personality and Social Psychology* 4, no. 2 (1966): 195–202, doi: 10.1016/0022-1031(74)90053-5.
9. Edwin A. Harris, Edwin F. Burtt, and Harold E. Fleishman, "Leadership and supervision in industry: An evaluation of a supervisory training program," *Bureau of Educational Research Monograph,* no. 33 (1955): 58, retrieved from https://babel.hathitrust.org/cgi/pt?id=mdp.39015049029807;view=1up;seq=76
10. C. Shawn Burke, Kevin C. Stagl, Cameron Klein, Gerald F. Goodwin, Eduardo Salas, and Stanley M. Halpin, "What type of leadership behaviors are functional in teams? A meta-analysis," *The Leadership Quarterly* 17, no. 3 (2006): 297–299, doi: 10.1016/j.leaqua.2006.02.007.

Chapter Five

1. Paul W. Atkins and Robert E. Wood, "Self- Versus Others' Ratings as Predictors of Assessment Center Ratings: Validation Evidence for 360-Degree Feedback Programs," *Personnel Psychology* 55, no. 4 (2002): 884, doi: 10.1111/j.1744-6570.2002.tb00133.x.
2. Simon Beausaert, Mien Segers, Didier Fouarge, and Wim Gijselaers, "Effect of using a personal development plan on learning and

development," *Journal of Workplace Learning* 25, no. 3 (2013): 149–152, doi: 10.1108/13665621311306538.

3. Phillippa Lally, Cornelia H. M. van Jaarsveld, Henry W. W. Potts, and Jane Wardle, "How are habits formed: Modelling habit formation in the real world," *European Journal of Social Psychology* 40, no. 6 (2009): 1002, doi:10.1002/ejsp.674.
4. Robert Hurling, Michael Catt, Marco De Boni, Bruce W. Fairley, Tina Hurst, Peter Murray, Alannah Richardson, and Jaspreet S. Sodhi, "Using Internet and Mobile Phone Technology to Deliver an Automated Physical Activity Program: Randomized Controlled Trial," *Journal of Medical Internet Research* 9, no. 2 (2007): 6–7, doi: 10.2196/jmir.9.2.e7.

Chapter Eight

1. William R. Miller and Stephen Rollnick, *Motivational Interviewing: Preparing People for Change,* 2nd ed. (New York: The Guilford Press, 2002), 13–14.
2. John A. Cunningham, Linda C. Sobell, Mark B. Sobell, and Janet Gaskin, "Alcohol and Drug Abusers' Reasons for Seeking Treatment," *Addictive Behaviors* 19, no. 6 (1994): 693, doi: 10.1016/0306-4603(94)90023-X.
3. Heidi M. Levitt, Ze'ev Frankel, Katherine Hiestand, Kimberly Ware, Karen Bretz, Rebecca Kelly, Sarah McGhee, Richard T. Nordtvedt, and Karina Raina, "The Transformational Experience of Insight: A Life-Changing Event," *Journal of Constructivist Psychology* 17, no. 1 (2004): 8, doi: 10.1080/10720530490250660.
4. Ola Svenson, "Are We All Less Risky and More Skillful Than Our Fellow Drivers?" *Acta Psychologica* 47, no. 2 (1981): 145, doi: 10.1016/0001-6918(81)90005-6.
5. Joyce Ehrlinger, Kerri Johnson, Matthew Banner, David Dunning, and Justin Kruger, "Why the Unskilled are Unaware: Further Explorations of (Absent) Self-Insight Among the Incompetent," *Organizational Behavior and Human Decision Making Processes* 105, no. 1 (2008): 105, 134, doi: 10.1016/j.obhdp.2007.05.002.
6. Peter H. Ditto and David F. Lopez, "Motivated Skepticism: Use of Differential Decision Criteria for Preferred and Nonpreferred Conclusions," *Journal of Personality and Social Psychology* 63, no. 4 (1992): 574–577, doi: 10.1037/0022-3514.63.4.568.
7. Timothy D. Ludwig and E. Scott Geller, "Improving the Driving Practices of Pizza Deliverers: Response Generalization and Moderating Effects of Driving History," *Journal of Applied Behavior Analysis* 24, no. 1 (1991): 32–41, doi: 10.1901/jaba.1991.24-31.
8. Jonathan L Freedman and Scott C. Fraser, "Compliance Without Pressure: The Foot-In-The-Door Technique," *Journal of Personality and Social Psychology* 4, no. 2 (1966): 195–202, doi: 10.1016/0022-1031(74)90053-5.

9. Joan F. Brett and Leanne E. Atwater, "360 Feedback: Accuracy, Reactions, and Perceptions of Usefulness," *Journal of Applied Psychology* 86, no. 5 (2001): 934–937, doi: 10.1037//0021-9010.86.5.930.
10. Stephen Rollnick and Jeff Allison, "Motivational Interviewing," in *The Essential Handbook of Treatment and Prevention of Alcohol Problems*, eds. Nick Heather and Tim Stockwell (West Sussex, England: John Wiley & Sons, 2004), 112.
11. Sune Rubak, Annelli Sandbæk, Torsten Lauritzen, and Bo Christensen, "Motivational interviewing: a systematic review and meta-analysis," *British Journal of General Practice* 55, no. 513 (2005): 307–309.
12. Elliot Aronson, Carrie Fried, and Jeff Stone, "Overcoming Denial and Increasing the Intention to Use Condoms through the Induction of Hypocrisy," *American Journal of Public Health* 81, no. 12 (1991): 1636–1637, doi: 10.2105/AJPH.81.12.1636.
13. Jeff Stone, Elliot Aronson, A. Lauren Crain, Matthew P. Winslow, and Carrie B. Fried, "Inducing Hypocrisy as a Means of Encouraging Young Adults to Use Condoms," *Personality and Social Psychology Bulletin* 20, no. 1 (1994): 121, doi: 10.1177/0146167294201012.

Chapter Nine

1. Carlo C. DiClemente and Mary M. Velasquez, "Motivational Interviewing and the Stages of Change," in *Motivational Interviewing: Preparing People for Change*, 2nd ed., eds. William R. Miller and Stephen Rollnick (New York: The Guilford Press, 2002), 201.
2. Johannes Thrul, Alexandra B. Klein, and Danielle E. Ramo, "Smoking Cessation Intervention on Facebook: Which Content Generates the Best Engagement?" *Journal of Medical Internet Research* 17, no. 11 (2015): e246–e249, doi: 10.2196/jmir.4575.
3. Rikki K. Wheatley, Richard P. West, Cade T. Charlton, Richard B. Sanders, Tim G. Smith, and Mathew J. Taylor, "Improving Behavior through Differential Reinforcement: A Praise Note System for Elementary School Students," *Education and Treatment of Children* 32, no. 4 (2009): 557–566.
4. Stefanie Ashford, Jemma Edmunds, and David P. French, "What Is the Best Way to Change Self-efficacy to Promote Lifestyle and Recreational Physical Activity? A Systematic Review with Meta-analysis," *British Journal of Health Psychology* 15, no. 2 (2010): 277, doi: 10.1348/135910709X461752.
5. See note 4 above.
6. Robert Hurling, Michael Catt, Marco De Boni, Bruce W. Fairley, Tina Hurst, Peter Murray, Alannah Richardson, and Jaspreet S. Sodhi, "Using Internet and Mobile Phone Technology to Deliver an Automated Physical Activity Program: Randomized Controlled Trial," *Journal of Medical Internet Research* 9, no. 2 (2007): 6–7, doi: 10.2196/jmir.9.2.e7.
7. See note 4 above.

8. See note 4 above.
9. Phillippa Lally, Cornelia H. M. van Jaarsveld, Henry W. W. Potts, and Jane Wardle, "How are habits formed: Modelling habit formation in the real world," *European Journal of Social Psychology* 40, no. 6 (2009): 1002, doi:10.1002/ejsp.674.
10. See note 9 above.

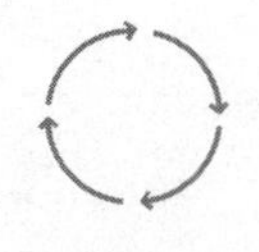

INDEX

active listening, 55, 57, 164–166
addiction treatment, 188
Aesop, 183
agreement, finding areas of, 141, 144
allocating
  appropriate time for tasks, 102, 104
  authority, 148–150
always questions, 194–195
Ambitious (personality trait), 57–58, 89, 106, 112, 115, 121, 128, 134, 139, 142, 146, 170
ambitious leaders, 57
American Psychologist, 8, 11
analyzing information, 53, 113–116
anticipating
  reactions, 138, 140
  threats, 133–134
Applied Behavior Analysis, 67
argument-counterargument cycle, 189–190, 200–201
Arizona State University, 186–187
artificial cues, 33
automaticity, 5, 24–25, 28, 34, 36, 37*f,* 74, 215
  beneficial nature of, 9–12
  and practice, 14–15, 15*f*
  of routines, 7–9
avoiding analysis paralysis, 120–123

bad habits, 6–7, 70
  benefits of, 202–204
  substituting incompatible behaviors for, 204–207
bad leaders, 5–7
behavioral change, 219
behavior analysts, 76
behavior(s), 23–24, 219
  consistent, 28–29
  habits from, 96
  incompatible, 205–206
  individual, 28–29
  in Leader Habit Formula, 27–29
  micro-, 29, 31, 35, 40, 67–69, 79, 84–85, 90, 93–94, 205–207
  new, 208–209, 215–216
  patterns of, 49–50
  related, 76–78
  simple, 28–29
bold goals, setting, 111–112
born leaders, 13
brain, 4–5, 8–9, 15–16, 74–75, 216
brainstorming solutions, 117–119, 130, 132
Brandon Hall Group, 17
breaking down projects, 102, 104
building strategic relationships, 158–161
building team spirit, 56, 154–157

Caring (personality trait), 55–56, 89, 109, 124–125, 150, 153, 156, 159, 161–163, 165

caring leaders, 55
chaining, 67–69
change, motivating, *see* motivating change
charisma, speaking with, 56, 169–171
chunking, 28
Cilley, Marla, 63, 73
clear rationale for tasks, 102, 105
close-ended questions, 164
coaching, 148–154
coaching leader habits, 197–220
  and bad habits, 202–207
  continued practice, 215–216
  in people contemplating change, 199–202
  and supporting habit-building efforts, 216–219
  supporting practice, 207–212
  through encouragement, 212–214
cognitive cues, 95
collaborative problem-solving, 144, 147
communicating, 56, 161–163, 166–169
competency, 215
conscious processing power, 8, 9, 12
consistent behaviors, 28–29
contemplation stage, 201–204, 218
context effect, 74
contingency plans, 133–135
continued practice, 215–216
core leadership skills, 13–14, 14*f*
creating urgency, 57, 110–113
critical feedback, 189–190, 192–193, 195, 213
Csíkszentmihályi, Mihály, 46–47
cue-behavior bond, 24–25, 34, 95–96
cue–behavior–reward, as full habit cycle, 26–27
cues, 11, 67, 84–85, 205–207, 219
  artificial, 33
  cognitive, 95
  effective behavioral, 32–35
  event-based, 22, 35
  good, 34
  individual, 28
  locational, 23–24, 73–75
  natural, 33, 35, 94–95
  and rewards, 31
Curious (personality trait), 53–54, 103–104, 115, 118, 121, 124–125, 131
curious leaders, 53
customers, 123–126
customer service, 123, 126

decisions, making good, 54, 55, 57, 113, 119–123
delegating, 55, 68, 108–110
deliberate practice, 4, 19, 24–25, 48, 95, 208–209, 218
developing leadership skills, 65–81
  with chains of micro-behaviors, 67–69
  with keystone habits, 70–73
  and locational cues, 73–75
  with related behaviors, 76–78
  and task- vs. people-oriented skills, 78–81
Duhigg, Charles, 69
Duke University, 32

EAR (Expectation—Action—Result), 209–212, 210*f,* 219
Ebbinghaus, Hermann, 18
empowering others, 56, 148–151
encouraging responsibility, 148, 150–151
event-based cues, 35
extrinsic rewards, 38, 53

facilitating reflection, 152, 154
feedback, 88
  critical, 189–190, 192–193, 195, 213
  negative, 71
  providing immediate and specific, 152–154
flow, 46–48
"Flow, the Secret to Happiness" (Csíkszentmihályi), 46
focusing on customers, 113, 123–126

focusing on people, 79–81, 86–90, 91*f*, *see also* Growing People & Teams; Interpersonal Skills; Persuasion & Influence
forgetting curve, 18
The Fox and the Grapes (Aesop), 183
full habit cycle, cue–behavior–reward as, 26–27

getting things done, 79–81, 86–90, 91*f*, *see also* Leading Change; Planning & Execution; Solving Problems & Making Decisions
goals
  clarifying team, 155, 157
  highlighting shared, 141, 144
  highlighting similar, 158, 160
  long-term, 127–129
  setting bold, 111–112
good cues, 34
great leaders, 12–16
Griffith University, 13
Growing People & Teams (skill set), 14*f*, 148–157
  and building team spirit, 154–157
  and empowering others, 148–151
  and mentoring and coaching, 151–154

habit cycle, 219
habits, 15*f*
  as automatic behaviors, 4–5
  bad, 6–7, 70
  bad vs. positive, 4
  from behaviors, 96
  formation of, 23–29, 36–38, 40–41, 74, 220
  positive, 4
Heath, Chip, 63
Heath, Dan, 63
Human Resources (HR), 10, 220
hypocrisy induction, 193–195, 208

incompatible behaviors, 205–206
individual behaviors, 28–29
ineffective leaders, 17, 30, 70
influencing others, 93, 94, 138–141
initiating relationships, 158, 160
innovating, 54, 55, 126, 129–132
internal tension, 180, 185, 189, 192–195, 218
Interpersonal Skills, 14*f*, 157–171
  and building strategic relationships, 158–161
  and communicating clearly, 166–169
  and listening actively, 164–166
  and showing caring, 161–163
  and speaking with charisma, 169–171
interrupting, 6–7
interviewing, motivational, 188–193, 196
intrinsic rewards, 38–40, 48, 49, 53, 59–60, 64
intuition, 11

just-in-time exercises, 94, 95

Kent State University, 184
key points, 166, 168
keystone habits, 69–74, 79–81, 84–85, 92
Kundera, Milan, 11

Laura (ER nurse), xi–xiv, 70, 94, 182, 189–192, 194
Leader Habit Formula, 3, 19, 21–41, 61, 207, 219–220
  effective behavioral cues in, 32–35
  habit formation in, 23–29
  practice in, 35–36, 37*f*, 207–212
  rewards in, 37–40
  skills in, 29–31
Leader Habit Quiz, 51, 52
Leader Habit Workout, 83–97
  and choosing your first exercise wisely, 84–85
  and danger of individual development plans, 91–92
  exercises in, 93–96

Leader Habit Workout (*cont.*)
identifying leadership skills for, 85–90, 91*f*
tracking your progress in, 96–97
leaders
ambitious, 57
bad, 5–7
born, 13
caring, 55
curious, 53
effective, 13–16, 30, 68, 79–81
great, 12–16
ineffective, 17, 30, 70
organized, 54
outgoing, 56
resilient, 58
leadership, genetic vs. learned factors in, 13
leadership development, 16–20, 188
leadership skill(s)
analyzing information as, 53, 113–116
core, 13–14, 14*f*
creating urgency as, 57, 110–113
customer focus as, 113, 123–126
decisions making as, 54, 55, 57, 113, 119–123
delegating as, 55, 68, 108–110
development stages of, 15*f*
innovation as, 54, 55, 126, 129–132
managing priorities as, 54, 102–105
managing risk as, 126, 132–135
and personality traits, 85, 88–90
planning/organizing work as, 105–108
selling the vision as, 56, 57, 126–129
speaking with charisma as, 56, 169–171
thinking through solutions as, 53, 55, 113, 116–119
see also specific skill sets
Leading Change (skill set), 14*f*, 126–135
and innovating, 129–132
and managing risk, 132–135
and selling the vision, 127–129
learned leadership, 13
learning, 18–19, *see also* over-learning
LinkedIn, 18
listening, active, 55, 57, 164–166
live leadership simulations, 30–31
locational cues, 73–75
long-term goals, 127–129
loudly, speaking, 7

Maastricht University, 60, 91
master project plans, 105, 107
mastery, 15*f*, 16, 25, 215–216, 219
memory, 18
mentoring, 56, 151–154
micro-behaviors, 29, 31, 35, 40, 67–69, 79, 84–85, 90, 93–94, 205–207
Miller, William R., 176, 188
motivating change, 175–196
and critical feedback, 183–190
and developing internal tension, 193–195
motivational interviewing, 188–193
and overcoming addiction, 176–180
in the unskilled, 181–183
motivational interviewing, 188–193, 196
music education, 19

natural cues, 33, 94–95
negative feedback, 71
negotiating, 57, 58, 144–147
neural circuits, 5
neurons, 4
never questions, 194–195
new behaviors, 208–209, 215–216
New York University, 6
next steps, seeking agreement on, 145, 147
nurses, 11

open-ended questions, xii–xiii, 164–166

Organized (personality trait), 54–55, 89, 103–104, 106, 109, 118, 121, 131, 134, 150, 168
organized leaders, 54
Outgoing (personality trait), 56–57, 89, 128, 142–143, 146, 159, 165, 168, 170
outgoing leaders, 56
overcoming individual resistance, 58, 141–144
over-learning, 15*f*, 16, 25, 36, 216, 219

patterns of behavior, 49–50
people-oriented leadership, 78–81, 86–90
personality trait assessment, 52*f*
personality trait(s), 48–58
  Ambitious as, 57–58, 106, 112, 115, 121, 128, 134, 139, 142, 146, 170
  Caring as, 55–56, 109, 124–125, 150, 153, 156, 159, 162, 165
  Curious as, 53–54, 103–104, 115, 118, 121, 124–125, 131
  Organized as, 54–55, 103–104, 106, 109, 118, 121, 131, 134, 150, 168
  Outgoing as, 56–57, 128, 142–143, 146, 159, 165, 168, 170
  Resilient as, 58, 118, 121, 139, 142–143, 146
Persuasion & Influence (skill set), 14*f*, 137–147
  and influencing others, 138–141
  and negotiating well, 144–147
  and overcoming individual resistance, 141–144
pilot testing, 133–135
pitch meetings, 10
planning and organizing work, 54, 105–108
Planning & Execution (skill set), 14*f*, 101–113
  and creating urgency, 110–113
  and delegating well, 108–110
  and managing priorities, 102–105
  and planning and organizing work, 105–108
The Power of Habit (Duhigg), 69
practice, 97
  and automaticity, 14–15, 15*f*
  and your brain, 15–16
  continued, 215–216
  deliberate, 4, 19, 24–25, 48, 95, 208–209, 218
preparation exercises, 93
priorities, managing, 54, 102–105
probing questions, 164, 166
processing power, 8, 9, 12
proficiency, 15*f*, 16, 208
progress tracking/monitoring, 105, 107–108, 148, 151
projects, matching, to skills and interests, 110

questions
  always, 194–195
  close-ended, 164
  never, 194–195
  open-ended, xii–xiii, 164–166
  probing, 164, 166
  targeted, 138, 140

reading, 8–9
reflection exercises, 94
related behaviors, 76–78
relationship-building skills, 158–161
relevant information, including only, 166–169
Resilient (personality trait), 58, 118, 121, 139, 142–143, 146
resilient leaders, 58
resources, identifying and creatively using, 105, 107
rewards, 25
  extrinsic, 38
  intrinsic, 38–40
risk, managing, 126, 132–135
root causes, uncovering, 138, 140
routines, 7–9

self-assessment baseline, 86–88, 87*f*
self-efficacy, 72–73, 84, 89–90, 92, 212–214, 219
self-help market, 16
self-image, 77–78, 179–181, 185–187, 189, 190, 192, 194, 208–209, 218
selling the vision, 56, 57, 126–129
simple behaviors, 28–29
simulated business scenarios, 84
skills, leadership, *see* leadership skill(s)
Skinner, B. F., 25–26
Solving Problems & Making Decisions (skill set), 14*f*, 113–126
  and analyzing information, 114–116
  and focusing on customers, 123–126
  and making good decisions, 119–123
  and thinking through solutions, 116–119
speaking
  with charisma, 56, 169–171
  loudly, 7
Stanford University, 77
"stop doing that" approach, 204–205
sustaining practice, 45–64
  and avoiding procrastination, 61–63
  by getting in the flow, 46–48
  by minimizing difficulty, 64
  by minimizing effort, 59–61
  and personality traits, 48–58
Switch (Heath and Heath), 63

targeted questions, 138, 140
task-oriented leadership, 78–81, 86–90
team-building, 155–157
team cohesion, 155–156
team goals, clarifying, 155, 157
TEDxYouth talks, 45–46
thinking through solutions, 53, 55, 113, 116–119
training, 17–19
transformational insights, 179–180
transformative insights, 181, 188–189, 192
twin studies, 13

"The Unbearable Automaticity of Being" (article), 8, 11
The Unbearable Lightness of Being (Kundera), 11
underlying issues, understanding, 119–122
Unilever Corporate Research, 96
University of Alberta, 61–63
University of Barcelona, 59
University of California at Santa Cruz, 193
University of Central Florida, 80
University of Helsinki, 49
University of Memphis, 179
University of New South Wales, 86
University of Oregon, 181
University of Southern California, 7
University of Stirling, 73
University of Sydney, 86
University of Tromso, 33
University of Virginia, 50
unskilled workers, 181–183, 187–188

Virginia Polytechnic Institute, 76
vision, 15–16, 56, 57, 127–129

weaknesses, 15, 15*f*
win-win opportunities, 158, 160–161
win-win solutions, 144, 146–147

zanshin, 47
Zhuangzi, 47